Privatisation of Municipal Finance in India

Privatisation of Municipal Finance in India

Janak Raj Gupta

ATLANTIC

PUBLISHERS & DISTRIBUTORS (P) LTD

Published by

ATLANTIC

PUBLISHERS & DISTRIBUTORS (P) LTD

7/22, Ansari Road, Darya Ganj,
New Delhi-110002
Phones : +91-11-23273880, 23275880, 23280451
Fax : +91-11-23285873
Web : www.atlanticbooks.com
E-mail : info@atlanticbooks.com

Branch Office
5, Nallathambi Street, Wallajah Road,
Chennai-600002
Phones : +91-44-64611085, 32413319
E-mail : chennai@atlanticbooks.com

ISBN 978-81-269-1051-9

Printed in India at Nice Printing Press, A-33/3A, Site-IV, Industrial Area, Sahibabad, Ghaziabad, U.P.

Preface

Municipal bodies designed as self-governing institutions have certain functional responsibilities and financial powers mandated by the respective municipal acts. Unlike other governmental institutions, they have both revenue-raising and expenditure responsibilities. In the post-independence period, there had been a steady decline in the functioning of urban local governments due to lack of finance which undermined their significance in the process of national development.

The existing institutional arrangement for the provision of essential services like water supply, garbage collection and disposal, primary health care, upkeep and maintenance of roads and street lighting, among others, are grossly inadequate, overstretched and overstrained. In a country with a large and increasing population and rapid urbanisation, the government is unable to cope up with the mounting pressure to maintain municipal services. The non-payment of service charges has weakened the institutional capacities to provide adequate levels of services. Privatisation of municipal finance is perhaps the only answer to these persistent problems.

Privatisation received a big push in India after the adoption of policy of liberalisation during the 1990s and has slowly and steadily spread to the level of local self-government in general and urban local bodies (ULBs) in particular. Many ULBs are reported to have privatised the collection of revenue from certain sources and provision of some services. In this context, a particular mention can be made of the collection of octroi, urban wastes management including landfills, maintenance of street lighting, municipal parks, pavements, toilets, etc.

The book *Privatisation of Municipal Finance in India* attempts to examine the changes in revenue collection and operational efficiency of different municipal services after privatisation in urban local bodies of some selected States. The study is based on the secondary data/information and field surveys conducted in States like Punjab, Haryana, Uttarakhand, Himachal Pradesh, Andhra Pradesh and Karnataka.

The book also presents an in-depth study of positive impacts of privatisation of urban wastes management based on field surveys of places like Suryapet and Greater Visakhapatnam (AP), Namakkal (TN), Bangalore (Kar) and SAS Nagar (Pb). The results based on the study of these places are, however, universally applicable in the country.

The book is based on the study conducted with the help of funds provided by the UGC under the award 'Emeritus Fellowship' granted to me in August 2005 for two years. I am naturally beholden to the UGC for the financial assistance and the honour bestowed on me. Thanks are also due to the Department of Economics, Punjabi University, Patiala, for providing me the necessary facilities to carry out this project.

I will be failing in my duty if I do not put on record the help rendered by the administrative and other staff of various Municipalities and Municipal Corporations. Specific thanks are due to the Director, Urban Local Bodies (Punjab) and various municipal bodies, viz. Malerkotla, Pathankot, Zirakpur, Mohali (SAS Nagar), etc. I am also thankful to the Commissioners, Municipal Corporation, Bengaluru (Karnataka);

Greater Visakhapatnam (A.P.); Dehradun (Uttarakhand); Panchkula (Haryana); Shimla (H.P.); Ludhiana and Patiala (Punjab); and to the Deputy Director, Regional Centre for Urban and Environmental Studies, Osmania University, Hyderabad. Special thanks are due to Mr. Joga Rao, Research Scholar (Andhra University, Visakhapatnam), for his unstinting help in conducting the survey on Urban Waste Management in Visakhapatnam. Thanks are also due to Mr. Raj Kumar for ungrudgingly typing the various drafts of the manuscript.

Although I have kept it to the end to thank my wife Bimla, it is not for the sake of ritual that I am doing so. Her support and sacrifice meant a great deal to the successful completion of this project.

Janak Raj Gupta

Contents

Preface *v*

1. Introduction 1

2. Privatisation of Revenue Collection 13
   Privatisation of Octroi 13
   Privatisation of Property Tax 20

3. Privatisation of Urban Waste Management/ Sanitation 28
   Suryapet in Andhra Pradesh 35
   Namakkal in Tamil Nadu 51
   Greater Visakhapatnam Municipal Corporation 57
   Bengaluru Mahanagar Palika (Karnataka) 73
   Sanitation in SAS Nagar/Mohali (Punjab) 81

4. Privatisation of Street Lighting and Other Services 90

5. Urban Development Schemes 98

6. Summary and Recommendations 120

Appendix 126

References 130

Introduction

1

Municipal bodies designed as self-governing institutions are endowed with certain functional responsibilities and financial powers mandated by the respective municipal acts. Unlike the other governmental institutions, they have both—revenue raising and expenditure responsibilities. But, in the post-independence period in India, there had been a steady decline in the functioning of the urban local governments undermining their significance in the national development process. While the fast growing urban areas across the country brought out several problems like increased demand for vital civic services against the limited infrastructure, growing slums and poverty and environmental pollution, the functional deterioration of the municipal bodies has become a critical factor. The Constitution 74th Amendment Act (74th CAA) assumes importance against this urban backdrop. The 74th CAA aims to revitalise the municipal bodies in terms of their democratic set-up, functional and financial powers, decentralised local governance and citizen-administration interface. Several measures—statutory, administrative and functional are necessary to realise the objectives of the 74th CAA at the state and local levels. During the past nearly one and a half decades after the 74th CAA, the state governments have taken several measures to implement its various provisions through conformity legislations and administrative follow-up.

It is a common knowledge that the existing institutional arrangement for the provision of essential services like water supply, garbage collection and disposal, primary health, road upkeep and maintenance, and street lighting in the urban areas are grossly inadequate, overstretched and overstrained. In a number of urban areas, the arrangements have virtually collapsed, with the result that a significant number of urban households, are forced to manage either with very inadequate levels of services or no services at all. The main reason may be that the institutions which are responsible for the provision of services came into being at a time when the pressure of urbanisation and urban growth was low. In the present scenario within which the institutions have to provide these services is very different. The population of urban areas has increased in recent years at rapid rates, and this has made it extremely difficult for the Urban Local Bodies (ULBs) to maintain, let alone expand and augment, the supply of services. During 1961-91, urban population in the country, for instance, increased by over 250 per cent; comparatively, the increase in the supply of services was insignificant although heavy investments were made in some of the services.[1]

The rapid increase in urban population is not the only factor that has strained the institutional capacities; a related factor is that a part of the urban population—in fact, a significant part, is either not able to pay or does not pay for the services that they use. While precise estimates on the number of such population are not available; there is no escaping the fact that the non-payment of service charges has weakened the institutional capacities in terms of their being able to provide adequate levels of services. Nobody realises the fact that the non-payment of user charges harm the users themselves in the long run. The ULBs or the institutions of self-governance can incur the fixed costs. But so far as the operational and other current charges are concerned, these must be covered from the users so as to run the service on an efficient line. Under the present changed circumstances, it is also argued that there is no justification for continuing with the same institutional set-up. Pressures of population, obsolete technology of services, and the rapidly changing demand profile of consumers have rendered the present set-up obsolete and irrelevant.[2]

If we review the overall situation with respect to the availability of services in the urban areas, many of these assertions would seem to be valid. In 1985, for which countrywide data are available, 27.1 per cent of India's total urban population had no access to safe drinking water, and 71.6 per cent had no access to basic sanitation. In many States such as Bihar, Andhra Pradesh, Assam, Orissa and Rajasthan, the proportions of population without these services were much higher. Also, the accessibility percentages do not mean that the services were either quantitatively adequate or qualitatively satisfactory. According to the studies on the subject, there are very few cities that are able to supply water at norms that are considered desirable on health considerations. In 20 per cent of cities with over 1,00,000 population, per capita supplies are less than 50 litres per day—a bare 24 per cent of what might be considered to be a desirable norm. The position with respect to the collection and disposal of garbage—one of those services that has high negative externalities, is worse; apart from the low population coverage by garbage collection services, on an average, 28 per cent of the garbage is left in the city streets uncollected, the impact of which on environment and health is beginning to pose a serious problem in a large number of urban areas. The inadequacies of municipal services are felt by the low income and urban poor households, who normally inhabit the poorly kept localities.[3]

An examination of the financial resources of the municipal bodies shows that the resources at their disposal are scarce, and barely increasing. During 1979-80 through 1983-84, the revenue incomes of the municipal bodies increased by 9.2 per cent as against this, the revenue expenditure increased by 56.2 per cent. Per capita expenditure (at 1986-87 prices) on municipal services was 64 per cent of the desirable expenditure norms and standards. In most of the class I cities (with population of more than 1,00,000) the per capita expenditure were below the norm.[4]

Given this general situation, the question arises as to what should be done to improve the access of urban population to basic urban services. Should we still continue to rely on the existing institutions such as the municipal bodies and other development board and departments or provide them some new alternatives? Should the private sector be brought in to replace or supplement or complement the net of existing institutions? It is important to mention at this stage that the question as to which agencies/institutions actually deliver and provide the various services and what their precise roles are, has not been systematically examined in literature.

It is assumed that the 'municipal bodies' (municipal corporations, municipalities and notified area committees) enjoy a kind of monopoly in respect of services such as water supply, waste disposal, sanitation, street lighting and road maintenance, etc. and that these services fall within their exclusive domain, with no role for other agencies. A survey of the urban areas would invalidate such a view, as there is a whole hierarchy of institutions within and outside the public domain, which are involved in the service provision. In addition to institutions in the public domain, there are a large number of private, formal and informal sector enterprises that play an important role in the provision of water. In other services like intra-city transport, health, education, the area of institutions involved in their provision is much wider. The urban services market, in this sense, is not simple or homogeneous, but highly complex and heterogeneous, presenting a situation where there are a few number of 'sellers' and a very large number of 'buyers'.[5]

The question of "who supplies what services", or a more difficult one, "who should supply what services" has traditionally been determined by one more consideration, i.e., the nature of the service. Why public agencies hold on to certain services without explicitly promoting or encouraging the private sector institutions, and why they prefer a secondary role, is determined to a significant extent by the nature of the service, i.e., whether it is a natural monopoly, or a merit good, or a pure public good or nearer to private good? The example of water supply is pertinent here as, it being a natural monopoly, the direct role of public agencies in the production, treatment and distribution has all through been dominant and visible. In other services which have no such dominant characteristics and where the externalities are not significant, the institutional network is evidently more complicated. Here too, the traditional way of dividing the public-private roles has undergone a major change, and it is no longer uncommon to have the private enterprise in natural monopolies or the public sector ownership in services that have no element of a merit/pure public goods.

It is necessary to bear in mind that the participation of the private sector has come about as a result of the growing dissatisfaction with the public provision. It has also made its entry in areas and spheres where a need was felt to supplement the publicly provided services. It does not necessarily follow from the above that the weaknesses of the public sector are a natural strength of the private sector. Nor should it be taken as the principal justification for involving the private sector in a major way. The private participation must come from within its own strength, and not from the weaknesses of the older existing systems.

It is a true fact that provision of services in the Indian cities and towns is a complex and challenging task. The public sector institutions continue to be the major providers of basic services such as water supply, street lighting, sanitation and waste collection and disposal although they are unable to provide the services satisfactorily. The public sector is also indispensable, to some extent, in the Indian context where a significant proportion of the population is poor and is dependent on the publicly provided services. While there is no doubt that the poor have benefited from the existing institutional arrangements, the economic costs of doing so have been heavy. The government is increasingly finding it difficult to bear the burden of subsidisation and, therefore, there is an urgent need to consider remedial measures. At present, however, a general scenario of low level of urban services, both in quantity and quality, prevails.

The provision of urban services varies with size, function and also physical characteristics of the city. In general, the level of urban services is far from satisfactory and calls for serious and critical deliberations over the management options with particular reference to the following:

(a) To allow the present system to continue and make serious efforts to improve the operational, financial and managerial efficiency of the public sector;

(b) To reckon that the public sector has very limited capacity to improve and to transfer the task of urban service provision to the private sector;

(c) To promote competition between the public and private sectors in provision of all urban services; and

(d) To involve the private sector in urban services through management contracts under the exclusive purview of the public sector.

The assumptions underlying each of the above listed options differ. The first goes partly by the thesis that it is not feasible to shift to a new system and partly by a feeling that there is a scope for improving the existing system. On the contrary, the second option stipulates that the existing system has some inherent administrative and financial constraints, which cannot be overcome by any reform; hence a choice in favour of private sector becomes justifiable. The third option takes the position that an introduction of competition between the public and private sectors may give the necessary shake-up to the public system and stimulate it to be more dynamic. Finally, the last option assumes that the major failure of the public system lies not in laying out the services but in their subsequent management, especially in recovery of charges. The private sector may be invited to handle this aspect with its characteristic of efficiency.

Management Options for Provision of Public Services

The management options for the provision of urban services have to be service and city specific. In nutshell, it can be stated that the choice of the management options of whether to improve the existing system or opt for a new system must take into account the problems of the individual cities, the management capability, and the public response. Involving the private sector in urban services through contracting out or out-sourcing seems to a positive option.

Options for Private Provision of Services

Private involvement in municipal services may be distinguished under two broad categories:

(a) Those under which the private parties bear no financial/ commercial risk, namely the contract for provision of services, the management contract, and profit sharing system;

(b) Those in which the private party bears all or part of such risk, namely, the concession and the lease.

Operation Contracts

This type of legal arrangement is a contract with an enterprise for the provision of those well-defined services necessary for good operation of the services. The private enterprise may be contracted for operations such as the cleaning of streets, collection of household waste, maintenance of street lighting and maintenance of transportation vehicles, etc. Under this system, the enterprise is compensated for the specific task or is given a fixed fee. In this arrangement the municipality remains legally responsible for the service and continues to manage the service in its name and collect fees from the users. The contractor will often be given a remuneration proportional to the number of service-units furnished (length of sewers cleaned, household refuse tonnage collected, length of streets cleaned and maintenance of the number of street lighting points, etc.). Other compensation formulae can also be worked out.

Management Contracts

This contract is almost an extension of the above form of contract. The manager is charged with all the tasks connected with the delivery of the public service, including billing and collection of fees from users and is the employer of all personnel used in the service. The public authorities do not intervene in the management of the service but control the manager according to the provisions of the contract. In this form also, the public authority is legally responsible for the delivery of the service and bears all the financial/commercial risks. The manager's remuneration is composed generally of a fixed annual amount or a fixed proportion of the revenue collected.

Concessional Contracts

In this form of contract the public authority contracts out the delivery of a public service to a private enterprise under its own control, including all the costs and risks involved. In this arrangement the private contractors bears the start-up costs, e.g., construction of the network of pipes, purchase of equipment, etc. During the period of contract, the concessionary runs the services at his own risk and cost, chooses and controls the personnel necessary for the operation of the service, modernises the facilities at his own cost and also buys all the necessary tools and materials. The private enterprise is compensated directly for the start-up costs through collection of user fees. These fees permit them to cover the capital costs and make profit on their investment. Concessions are awarded for a long period of time. At the end of the concession period, the facilities become the property of the public authority.

The main advantage of this system is that it relieves the public authority of financial burdens while assuring efficient service. But the private enterprise may call upon the public authorities to support them when financial difficulties arise. Sometimes the private enterprise may be required to carry out investments for which no full cost recovery can be expected, or the public authority may be reluctant to allow an increase in rates. So, the public authority may be compelled to provide subsidies, give lower cost credits, etc. to allow the private enterprise to continue the service.

Lease System

In this arrangement the lessee receives already existing facilities and has to provide management and operation of the public service and advance only the operating funds. The lessee operates the public service at his own commercial risk by bearing deficits and benefiting from profits. Remuneration comes from fees which he levies on the users and payments are made to the lessor (public authority) to cover debt service or other costs relating to the financing of facilities, their renewal and extension. The lessee has the full legal responsibility to deliver the service and is at liberty to choose the technical means for the purpose.

The lease contract usually contains detailed provisions on setting and adjusting rates as well as on the exercise of control by the public entity over the operation of the service and over the account of the lessee. In this arrangement, the lessee does not make the initial investment to build the facilities, and so the contract is for a shorter duration as the lessee only brings in working capital which can balance the investment in a shorter period.

Joint Ventures

This is a system of association of public sector with the private sector. There are many possible ways through which such arrangement may be initiated. The public authority can create a joint venture with one or more private enterprises. It can then make a contract with this company under one of the system described above. The public authority may secure an interest in an existing company delivering a public service.

Under ideal circumstances, the joint venture should reconcile both the community/social and the private interest. While the rendering of the public service for profit is recognised, the profit aim is checked by the public service and nature of its activity. On the other hand, at least part of the profits must revert to the community.

Role of the National and State Governments

Many of the research studies highlighted the fact that, despite being a major provider of urban services, the public sector's ability to improve and augment the existing services is limited. The present institutional arrangement for delivery of urban services, though varied over the country, does not seem to be able to cope with the growing demand for urban services in the cities. In order to manage the demand for urban services concerted efforts on the part of the national and the state governments are necessary in the following areas:

(i) Financing of urban infrastructure;

(ii) Fiscal measures;

(iii) Strengthening the capacity of local governments; and

(iv) Legislative and institutional reforms.

Financing of Urban Infrastructure

One of the crucial aspects of urban services requiring intervention of the national government relates to financing of urban services. The total finances required for investments in core urban services have been estimated to be anywhere Rs. 25,000 crores (NCU report, 1989) to Rs. 40,000 crores (NIUA estimates). Investments even at the lower estimates, are beyond the present capacity of the urban local governments, through its internal means. The present institutional arrangement for financing urban infrastructure is also unlikely to cope with such a large requirement.

Central government has hitherto paid little attention to the requirements of the urban areas. In the absence of any support for urban area, it is quite likely that infrastructure bottlenecks will impede urban productivity and in turn affect the national growth as well. It is proposed that central government's role should be enhanced in financing urban infrastructure in the following two ways[6]:

1. Increasing plan allocation for urban infrastructure development through a programme on Integrated Urban Infrastructure Development. Under such a programme, efforts will have to be made to provide budgeting and extra-budgetary support to the tune of Rs. 1500 crores per annum for urban infrastructure investments.
2. Creation of a network of specialised financial institutions to meet the requirements of urban infrastructure. While the Seventh Five Year Plan had made an explicit provision for an Urban Infrastructure Bank, its implementation has been only as a window in the HUDCO (Housing and Urban Development Corporation). The total lending by HUDCO for urban infrastructure in the past couple of years has been on the increase, but it is nowhere near the required levels. In addition, the financial viability of the project and the debt servicing abilities of the local governments are also not given due importance under the present institutional systems.

In order to provide greater access to the urban local governments and the private sector enterprise that are likely to be promoted in provision of urban services, it is necessary for the central government to establish a specialised Urban Infrastructure

Finance Institution or create a mechanism for refinancing infrastructure lending by other financial institutions. The experiment in recent past, with regard to housing finance institutions, suggests, that it is possible to set up a commercially viable infrastructure finance institution within a short period of time, if the central government provides appropriate institutional support and adopts facilitative policies.

The requirements for urban infrastructure are large and varied both according to the nature of services as well as city size. The capacities of the local governments are also limited to formulate technically appropriate and financially viable projects. It is thus necessary to provide both technical support as well as financial support to the local bodies. A regional network of financing institutions that can work closely with the local governments is essential. At present, in each state there exists an industrial development corporation and industrial finance corporation. The professional skills available at these organisations may be utilised in the initial stages of establishing regional institutions.

Fiscal Measures

There is a significant role to be played by both the public and the private sectors in providing urban public services. However, for the private sector, the primary motive is of profit generation and unless conditions to this effect are created, it is unlikely that one would see a significant involvement of this sector in provision of urban services.

Thus in addition to the creation of financial institutions to which the private sector would also have access, it is necessary to provide some fiscal incentives to them as well.

Such fiscal incentives could be in the form of accelerated depreciation allowances, as has been done in case of energy conservation measures. Other possible incentives would be to introduce investment allowance schemes for capital investments in urban infrastructure by the private sector. These investment allowances may be offset against current profits of the enterprise.

The exact quantum of the above fiscal incentives would depend on their net effect on the rates of return on investments.

Such returns in turn are contingent upon appropriate pricing of urban public services. It is thus crucial to permit the local governments and the private enterprises involved in the delivery of urban public services, to levy appropriate prices to recover the costs of investments.

REFERENCES

1. National Institute of Urban Affairs, "Public-Private Provision of Urban Services", Research Study Series Number 50, New Delhi, Dec. 1992.
2. *Ibid.*
3. National Institute of Urban Affairs, "Management of Urban Services", Research Study Series No. 14, New Delhi, 1986.
4. National Institute of Urban Affairs, "Upgrading Municipal Services, Norms and Financial Implications", Vol. I, Research Study Series, No. 38, New Delhi, 1989.
5. National Institute of Urban Affairs, "Public-Private Provision of Urban Services", Research Study Series No. 5, New Delhi, Dec. 1982.
6. National Institute of Urban Affairs, "Public-Private Provision of Urban Services", Research Study Series No. 50, New Delhi, Dec. 1992.

Privatisation of Revenue Collection

2

Many ULBs have also tried successfully to privatise their revenue sources, notably octroi or entry tax collections. Even the collection of property tax has been seen to have improved by involving the stakeholders (property owners) in self-assessment of property tax.

PRIVATISATION OF OCTROI

The income from octroi is a major source of revenue for most of the municipal bodies in India. However, it has continued to be one of the most controversial taxes at the local level. A number of Committees and Commissions have identified octroi as a regressive, undesirable and anachronistic tax and have recommended for its abolition. In particular, it has been argued to cause severe harassment to the transporters as the trucks carrying goods and commodities have to stop at the octroi barriers for assessment of the tax. Some of the problems that are generally associated with the octroi are: (i) adverse impact on trade and commerce; (ii) waste of time and fuel at check-posts; (iii) regressive nature of the tax; (iv) undervaluation and corruption at all stages of collection; and (v) high collection cost. In spite of the limitations and drawbacks of the octroi as a tax, it plays a significant role in augmenting the municipal finance. Most of the Committees and Commissions, which have examined the issue of octroi abolition have perhaps not cared to appreciate the revenue importance of octroi and the adverse impact of the abolition on the much constrained state finances and municipal finances. Abolition of octroi has, therefore, to be viewed in the context of urbanisation process and the requirement to match the demographic growth and urban migration with augmentation of civic services and other facilities.

It may be mentioned that the new economic policies are aimed at stepping up of economic growth, improving market efficiency and competitiveness, and integrating the Indian economy with the global commodity markets. Such changes have significant implications for the different sectors of the economy especially the urban sector and cities where, most of the new investments are expected to be made. The likely increase in urban productivity and population will place a heavy demand on all kinds of urban infrastructure and services. The infrastructure bottlenecks in urban areas are likely to pose serious impediments in enhancing urban productivity. The municipal bodies are already under considerable strain to cope up with the maintenance of existing services not to speak of creating additional facilities and improving it. The revenue base of these local bodies has been eroding consistently, while their responsibilities for augmenting existing services has been growing.

Such a grim financial situation of municipal bodies does not permit to further allow the shrinking of their fiscal base. In some States octroi contributes about 60 to 70 per cent of the total tax revenues of the municipal bodies. Abolition of octroi thus has direct implications on municipal finances. So unless alternative sources of revenue are made available to the local bodies, the abolition of octroi will lead to great losses to the State and Local Governments. In the meantime, the octroi collection system could be improved through procedural and administrative reforms. Octroi collection can be privatised to plug the evasion in it and to reduce cost of octroi collection. Many state governments have taken a policy decision to invite private parties for octroi collection in order to improve the finances of local bodies and efficiency in the collection system. In Rajasthan, for example, a decision has been taken at the state government level, to hand over octroi collection to private agencies. The government decision does not, however, bind all the municipal bodies to switch over to the private contract system. According to Directorate of Local Bodies, Rajasthan, out of 181 municipal bodies, 35 have already accepted the scheme, and others are in the process of inviting quotations. The official sources revealed that the collection for each municipal bodies, might be increased at least two to three times through such system. For instance, the Bikaner Municipal Council, which was the first one to switch over to the private contract system, the bid amount was quoted for Rs. 12 crores, which was three times higher than the collection by the municipality.

It may be mentioned that normally there is no change in the rate of octroi during the period of contract. However, the exemptions announced by the government from time to time continue to be applicable to the private agencies concerned.

Terms and Conditions for Giving Collection of Octroi for Contract

The terms and conditions for giving collection of octroi to private hands are almost similar for each municipality in Punjab, but each municipality can make minor changes according to its requirement:

1. The contract will be applicable for a specified period.
2. Each bidder has to deposit a pre-specified amount in cash/demand draft to the Executive Officer of the municipality before the start of bidding. Cheque is not accepted.
3. The reserve price of the contract is predetermined on the basis of the last year's collection.
4. If the bidding is to be given by a firm or company, then the proof for partnership and the person authorised by the firm or company will have to be submitted before the start of bidding.
5. Contractor/agent of the firm will have to sign an agreement with the municipality within 15 days on legal papers (ashtam) after the bidding, otherwise the amount deposited at the time of bidding will be forfeited.
6. Contractor has to deposit one-tenth of the total amount of the contract in cash or a bank guarantee from a nationalised bank within 15 days, otherwise the security amount will be forfeited.

7. Contractor can take the services of employees of municipality but he has to deposit money in advance at the rate of Rs. 3,000 for superintendent, Rs. 2,000 for inspector, Rs. 1,000 for clerk and Rs. 700 for peon.
8. The total amount of contract will be payable in 50 equal weekly installments.
9. The contract is not applicable to octroi on electricity and commodity subject to state excise duty and the municipality will get the octroi on liquor and electricity separately as earlier.
10. The income which the municipality earn from State transit, 10 per cent of it will be given to contractor as service charges and 90 per cent will be sent to the government.
11. Contractor cannot sublet the contract.
12. Contractor can use the existing octroi posts of the municipality or he may open new octroi post as per requirement. The arrangement of light, tables, chairs and stationery, etc., will be done by the contractor himself. But the printed stationery and other printed material will be provided by the municipality/council at his own expenditure.
13. Contractor/agent will collect the octroi for the specified period as per rules and orders of the municipality/government.
14. The collection of octroi will be done as per schedule and act/account code of the Punjab Government and prevailing rules of the municipality/council. If any change in the rate structure of octroi is done by the government, then the contractor will have to make the payment after negotiating with the municipality council. The contractor will have to follow the modifications done in the rules/bylaws by the government from time to time. If any person is caught doing octroi theft, executive officer of the council has the right to fix the fine or agreement fee.

15. If there is any fall in the collection of octroi due to natural calamities or strikes during the period of contract, the contractor will not get any relief.
16. If there is any dispute between the contractor and municipality/council at any stage, then the arbitrator will be the concerned Deputy Director Urban Local Bodies and his decision will be binding for both the parties. Contractor/agent will not go to civil court in any case.
17. If contractor appoints his employees, a list along with their addresses will be provided to the Executive Officer of the municipality. Identity cards will be provided by the municipality but the expenditure will be borne by the contractor/agent.
18. If contractor wants to take the help of police, then he can approach the police department through municipality and may take the police employees on deputation. But the contractor will be bound to deposit the amount of salaries and other allowances as per the conditions of police department for deputation to the municipality.
19. If octroi is abolished by the government at any stage or there is any modification in it, then the concerned contractor will be bound to follow the orders of the government.
20. The municipality will return the bank guarantee/ earnest money to the contractor after the completion of the contract within one month after clearing the account of collection of octroi and getting no-due certificates from the office.
21. If there is any increase in the boundary limit of the municipality, then the concerned contractor will be responsible to pay extra money after negotiations. The contract will be cancelled if the required modifications in the payable amount are not done.

Sometimes privatisation of octroi is objected on the ground that it will lead to retrenchment of the existing municipal staff.

Therefore, many municipalities include a clause relating to the retention of existing staff. For example, in case of Bikaner, state officials pointed out that as per the draft terms of reference, the private contractors will retain 30 per cent of the existing staff for the same duty whereas the remaining 70 per cent will be redeployed for other municipal works. Thus there will be no retrenchment in this system.

The Table 2.1 shows position of revenue collection of octroi before and after privatisation in selected municipalities in Punjab. The total collection from octroi in the selected municipalities of Punjab was Rs. 2836.24 lakhs during the year 1996-97 and within three years it increased to Rs. 6223.93 lakhs during the year 1999-2000 after privatisation. It means that revenue collection from octroi increased by 119 per cent after privatisation. The growth in the collection of octroi after privatisation was maximum in the case of Sahnewal 420 per cent and minimum in the case of Kartarpur (57%). The increase in the revenue collection from octroi was less than 100 per cent after privatisation for the municipalities of Jandiala (79%), Rayya (90%), Gobindgarh (78%), Hoshiarpur (93%), Kartarpur (57%) and Jagraon (98%). The growth in the collection from octroi was between 100 per cent and 200 per cent for most of municipalities.

The increase in the revenue collection from octroi was more than 200 per cent in case of municipalities: Ajnala (377%), Dinanagar (217%), Dhariwal (330%), Sahnewal (420%), Morinda (208%). There is no doubt that the revenue collection from octroi has increased after privatisation. One of the main reasons of increase in the collection of octroi after privatisation may be that earlier there was a large scale evasion in the octroi. But after privatisation, the contractor has tried to stop the evasion in the octroi.

However, it must be mentioned that although privatisation of octroi collection has many advantages yet it has to be handled cautiously. After privatisation of octroi some complaints of harassment by contractors were received. Thus strict vigil and monitoring is needed in this arrangement by the official agency concerned in order to avoid the above situation. It is accepted

Table 2.1. Collection of Octroi before and after Privatisation in Selected Municipalities in Punjab

(Rs. Lakhs)

Name of the Municipality	Before Privatisation (1996–97)	After Privatisation latest amount 1999–2000	Increase (Per cent)
Jandiala	29.27	52.28	79
Majitha	10.50	21.65	106
Ajnala	20.08	95.85	377
Rayya	25.40	48.20	90
Gurdaspur	84.67	253.64	200
Quadian	22.18	45.04	103
Pathankot	181.41	494.30	172
Dinanagar	36.46	115.45	217
Dariwal	17.78	75.10	330
Machhiwara	34.96	81.85	132
Kharar	54.51	121.10	122
Raikot	44.32	88.15	99
Sahnehwal	27.47	142.90	420
Kurali	54.88	135.00	146
Doraha	58.65	148.00	152
Mullanpur	21.57	56.05	160
Morinda	35.28	108.75	208
Samrala	30.32	63.05	108
Ropar	59.18	171.50	190
Malout	9.38	28.02	199
Gobindgarh	737.00	1315.00	78
Khanna	315.86	736.37	133
Hohiarpur	381.00	736.76	93
Kartarpur	32.30	50.71	57
Nakodar	76.02	152.00	100
Shahpur	37.50	76.00	103
Nawanshahr	84.91	183.08	116
Jagraon	110.00	218.00	98
Nurmahal	25.82	54.59	114
Batala	177.86	356.14	100
Total	2836.24	6223.93	119

Source: Directorate of Urban Local Bodies, Punjab.

that revenue from octroi has increased in almost all the municipalities after the contract system and on the other hand, expenditure on octroi staff and patrolling has substantially reduced. It has been reported that the Karyana Merchant's Association of Mohali has urged the municipal council, not to give octroi collection to private contractor. They allege that contractor's staff is mostly ill informed about the rules, which results in harassment of the people. Most of them are rude and all they want is to take as much money as possible from the people. While octroi rates vary from article to article, contractor's men mostly charge the maximum rates. They demand money on even those goods which are otherwise exempted from octroi. But ultimately consumers have to suffer as traders pass on the burden to them. Members of the Beopar Mandal said the employees of the contractor were not even aware of the rates at which the octroi had to be imposed on various items. They imposed their own rates and even misbehaved with residents.

The Gypsy-borne octroi collectors can often be seen chasing long-route vehicles and stopping them on the busy highway in a filmy style. This has often led to accidents. To stop a suspect motorist, the octroi collectors, often drive their vehicles on the wrong side of the highways, heightening the chances of accidents. The men employed by the octroi contractor have been using all possible means to meet their daily target of collection of money without caring for the inconvenience of the public. Cases of overcharging from passengers and motorists from far-flung areas have also come to light. Contractor's men even searched vegetable bags at the level crossing.

Certain affected families were of the view that the civic body should depute its own employees at every octroi post so that commuters were not overcharged or harassed by the contractor's men. These officials should be appointed in rotation to avoid the creation of vested interests. The telephone numbers, preferably mobile telephone numbers should be clearly displayed at each octroi post so that the victims could contact the municipal staff who can immediately ensure that genuine persons are not unduly harassed by the musclemen of the contractors.

PRIVATISATION OF PROPERTY TAX

Though strictly speaking privatisation of property tax may not be a feasible proposition, yet the involvement of stake-holders, i.e., property owners, in assessing the tax is one step short of privatisation. In this connection it would be interesting to study the property taxation system of Bengaluru Mahanagar Palike (BMP).

Taxation System in Bengaluru Mahanagar Palike (Karnataka)

The BMP had to introduce the new SAS (Self-Assessment System) under capital value system in view of the amendment to KMC Act, 1976. The taxation system of BMP can be studied in three parts:

Part I: Before implementation of SAS—prior to April 1, 2000.

Part II: SAS implemented from April 1, 2000.

Part III: New SAS under CVS.

Part I: Taxation System in BMP before Implementation of SAS

- Annual Rental Value (ARV) System.
- Probable rent which a property can fetch from month to month or year to year.
- No guidelines were issued for arriving at the ARV.
- Assessment was subject to official discretion.
- Similar buildings were being assessed at different rates resulting in citizen dissatisfaction.
- Actual rents were not being taken for assessment.
- False declaration of rent caused loss of revenue.
- Several courts have held to consider standard rent or fair rent on the basis of House Rent Control Act.
- Penalty on defaulters was only @ 5% p.a.

Part II: SAS Implemented from April 1, 2000

- SAS of property tax was optional since the Act was not amended by that time.
- Citizen friendly since it was based on fair and rational apartments.
- Transparent and simple for calculation of assessment of tax.
- The BMP was classified into six zones based on the guidance value per sq. ft. as given below:

a. Above Rs. 6000
b. Between Rs. 4000 and Rs. 6000
c. Between Rs. 2000 to Rs. 4000
d. Between Rs. 1000 to Rs. 2000
e. Between Rs. 500 and Rs. 1000
f. Below Rs. 500

Classification of Properties and Rebate under SAS

- Residential properties were classified into five categories based on the cost of construction.
- Non-residential properties were classified into 11 categories based on the usages and location.
- 50 per cent rebate was given for self-occupation both for residential and non-residential usage.

Features of SAS

- Depreciation for the building was introduced for the first time.
- Rates for arriving ARV was prescribed for each category of properties in different zones based on the cost of construction, location and usage.
- A commitment was made to the effect that the SAS would remain in force until March 31, 2005.
- Minimum and maximum increase of tax was fixed in case of abnormal increase or decrease (limited 2½ times of the existing tax in case of abnormal increase or 25 per cent decrease in case of abnormal decrease).
- 80 banks in different areas were authorised to accept payment of property tax.
- Provision for scrutiny of self-assessment declarations not exceeding 5 per cent of the total declarations received each year.

Impact

- Citizens of Bengaluru accepted the scheme.
- Hon'ble High Court and Supreme Court have upheld the scheme.

- More than 50 per cent of the property owners have paid their tax voluntarily.
- Increase of tax collection to Rs. 157.50 crores as against Rs. 117.50 crores collected during the previous year.
- General revision was given effect to for the remaining properties of those who did not opt for SAS, on the same rates of SAS.

Part III: New SAS under CVS—Main Features of the Amendment

- Self-assessment/declaration made compulsory.
- Market value guidelines of properties published by government under section 45 B of Karnataka Stamp Act, 1957, shall be considered (50%).
- Fifty per cent rebate is given for those who pay property tax within 30 days from the date of commencement of the year.
- Levy of penalty on the defaulters @ 2 per cent per month.
- Penalty of Rs. 100 in case of failure to submit the return after payment of property tax in full.
- No tax on vacant land around the building.
- Revision of tax once in 3 years.
- Payment of tax in only one installment—within 90 days from the date of commencement of the year.

Rates of Tax Prescribed in the Act

• Vacant Land:	
Below 1000 sq. mtr.	0.1 to 0.2%
Above 1001 sq. mtr. and below 4000 sq. mtr.	0.025 to 0.5%
Above 4001 sq. mtr.	0.01 to 0.02%
• Residential Buildings	0.3 to 1%
• Non-residential Buildings	0.5 to 2%

Proposed classification of properties (CVS)

Nine categories for the purpose of levying tax is as under:

1. Vacant Land
2. Residential properties
3. Non-residential properties (commercial)
4. Non-residential properties (semi-public)
5. Cinema Theaters
6. Kalyana Mantapas, Shaadi Mahal, etc.
7. Hospital and Industries (other than buildings of information technology)
8. Star Hotels
9. Levy of service charges on buildings exempted from payment of property tax.

Proposed rate of tax for vacant land in BMP

Category	Area	Multiplication Factor
A	Upto 1000 sq. mtr. (10764 sq. ft.)	0.1%
B	Between 1001 sq. mtr. and 4000 sq. mtr. (10765 to 43040 sq. ft.)	0.025%
C	Above 4001 sq. mtr. or 43041 sq. ft.	

Proposed rate of tax for Residential Buildings of BMP

Category	GV per sq. ft.	Rate of tax for building and land occupied by buildings	
		When built up area is equal or less than the sital area	When the built up area is more than the sital area
A	Below Rs. 1000	0.5%	0.6%
B	Rs. 1001 to Rs. 1500	0.4%	0.6%
C	Rs. 1501 and above	0.3%	0.6%
D	For apartments and flats	0.6%	0.6%

Proposed rate of tax for NR properties in BMP

	When built up area is equal or less than the sital area	When the built up area is more than the sital area
Category I NR properties (Commercial)	1% (0.001%)	2% (0.002%)
Category II Gym and Physical fitness centres where articles of food and/or liquor are not served, educational institutions, students' hostels, and other hospitals attached to medical colleges which are not exempted under section 110 or KMC Act	1% (0.01%)	1% (0.01%)

Proposed rate of tax for other NR categories in BMP

Category	Description	Rate of tax for the building and the land occupied by the building
1	Cinema theaters, industries (other than buildings of information technology)	0.6% (0.006%)
2	Kalyan Mantapas, Shaadi Mahals, Reception Halls, etc.	0.6% (0.006%)
3	Hospitals	0.8% (0.008%)
4	Star hotels	1.5% (0.015%)
Service charges on exempted properties		25% of the property tax

Benefits

- There were only six zones in SAS. Now every street will act as a zone since it will have its own guidance value.
- With the introduction of new SAS rationalisation, transparency and simplicity will be achieved.
- Self-declaration of property tax.
- Five per cent of rebate for those who pay property tax within 30 days from the date of commencement of the year.

Constraints

- By and large for a similar set of properties in terms of locations GV sital value the difference between old SAS and new SAS is marginal.

- However, there are certain exceptions. Although different rates for different category of properties have been proposed with a view to bring the difference between old SAS and new SAS to the minimum extent, yet there will be large variation in certain properties both in residential and NR properties.
- It cannot be compared with SAS.

Amendment Sought

Floor and cap method i.e., fixing of maximum and minimum rates in case of abnormal increase or decrease is required. If there is abnormal increase, the increase can be limited to 50 per cent of the existing tax. If there is abnormal decrease, the decrease can be limited to 25 per cent of the existing tax.

Collection of Property tax for the last five years (Rs. in Crores)

Year	Target	Achievements
1999-2000	120	117.50
2000-2001	150	157.50
2001-2002	175	162.50
2002-2003	200	195.00
2003-2004	250	200.00
2004-2005	250	230.00
2005-2006	300	260.00
2006-2007*	400	290.00

* Upto January 2007

Thus the experience of BMP shows that reposing faith in property owners i.e., self-assessment of property can greatly improve the property tax collections. Property tax collections nearly increased three times between 1999-2000 and 2006-07, i.e., after the self-assessment of property tax was made mandatory.

Property Tax, Urban Development and the Value of Property

It may be interesting to observe that since the value of property determines one's ability to pay tax, therefore, it may be significant to examine the relationship between value of property and property tax; and between Urban Development and Value of Property.

It has been found that value of property and property tax are inversely related, i.e., as property tax increases, value of property decreases and *vice versa*. Therefore, whenever the value of property is enhanced by spending more and more on urban infrastructure or by providing other urban amenities as is the case with Jawaharlal Nehru National Urban Renewable Mission (JNNURM), then the prospectus of raising more resources through property tax are enhanced. It should be remembered that enhanced value of property is unearned income/wealth, therefore, on equity ground also property tax should be made more progressive.

On the other hand, as higher property tax rates lower the value of property, therefore, the tax proceeds should be used to enhance the municipal infrastructure, thereby increasing the value of property to neutralise this adverse effect.

Further, in order to encourage municipalities to build infrastructure, some in-built mechanism to ensure regular and ever increasing transfer of resources to municipalities must be there. Ad hoc grants, even if substantial are not conducive to the growth of urban infrastructure.

Privatisation of Urban Waste Management/ Sanitation

3

According to projections made by the UNFPA *Report on the State of World Population* (2007) for the first time in history, more than half of the human population of the world, i.e., 3.3 billion people, will be living in urban areas. By 2030, the number will touch five billion. The report warns that many new urbanites will be poor. The report also warns that the history of attempts to control rural-urban migration flows is couched in frustration.

Urbanisation is now becoming a world-wide phenomenon. As per 2001 census, India's population reached 1027 million, out of which about 742 million live in rural areas and 285 million in urban areas. Percentage of urban population to total population of the country stands at 27.8. In 1991 census, this percentage was 25.7. An increase of 2.1 per cent has been recorded in the urban population during 1991-2001. The decadal growth of urban population during 1991-2001 is 31.2 per cent as against 36.4 per cent during 1981-1991. By 2011 and 2021, India's urban population is estimated to be 366 million and 459 million respectively, showing an increase of 81 million and 174 million as compared to 285 million in 2001. The National Capital Territory of Delhi is the most urbanised (93.0%) among all the states and Union Territories (35 in all) followed by Chandigarh (89.8%) and Pondicherry (66.6%) as per 2001 census. Among the major states, Tamil Nadu is the most urbanised state with 43.9 per cent of the population living in urban areas followed by Maharashtra (42.4%) and Gujarat (37.4%). The proportion of the urban population is the lowest in Bihar with 10.5 per cent followed by Assam (12.7%) and

Orissa (14.9%). Global experience shows that when a country's urban population reaches almost 25 per cent of the overall population (as in the case of India) the pace of urbanisation accelerates.[1]

The uncontrolled growth in urban areas has left many Indian cities deficient in infrastructural services such as water supply, sewerage and solid waste management. Various efforts, including privatisations, have been made to evolve a strategy for improvement in water supply and sanitation. However, sanitation was limited mostly to disposal of human excreta while solid waste management did not receive adequate attention. The continuing urbanisation due to various factors like demographic and economic changes, industrialisation, increase in density of population, is exerting immense pressure on the existing municipal wastes management services.

The term 'waste' implies that it is of no concern to anyone and is of no value. The intrinsic value of the material as a resource or as an object of further utility has not been fully recognised. "Solid Waste" is the term used to describe non-liquid waste material arising from domestic, trade, commercial, agricultural and industrial activities and from public services. In Indian cities, it is a combination of various heterogeneous waste materials. It is commonly known as garbage, refuse, rubbish or trash. Its main sources are residential premises, business establishments and street sweepings. It is a mixture of vegetable and organic matter, inert matter like glass, metal, stones, ashes, cinders, textiles, wood, grass, etc. Solid wastes arising from hospitals may be included too (bandages, syringes, empty bottles, etc.). A separate and exclusive treatment of hospitals solid waste management is needed.

The word waste is used for a discarded material, which has no consumer value to the person abandoning it. Solid waste is defined as 'material' for which the primary generator or user abandoning the material within the urban area requires no compensation upon abandonment. Insofar as urban solid waste is concerned, it is generally perceived by society as being within the responsibilities of the municipality to collect and dispose of.

Solid waste management involves the activities of management associated with generation, collection, transfer and transport, processing and disposal of solid waste which is environmentally compatible adopting principles of economy, aesthetics, energy and conservation. It encompasses planning, organisation, administration, economic and engineering aspects involving interdisciplinary relationships.

Global Perspectives on Solid Waste Management

Managing solid waste has become more and more a global business than just being a local concern because of its cross-border manifestations. The developed and developing nations are finding ways to reduce, recycle or reuse and dispose waste effectively to keep cities clean. All major cities have witnessed an enormous rise in generation of solid waste with changing urban pattern and life styles.

In this era, with garbage going global, there are several methods, technologies, approaches that have emerged to manage waste hygienically and sustainably. Waste management is an essential task, which has important consequences on public health, urban environment and the productivity of urban economy. Local authorities across the globe have started realising the magnitude of this pressing problem and have adopted innovative ways to solve their waste problems depending on availability of land, technology, financial and other resources.

European countries follow the principle of 'polluter pays' wherein the polluter should pay to collect and recycle all the waste material. These countries are actively encouraging energy recovery with thermal treatment which leads to reduction in landfill volume, some reduction in global warming gases.

The American system strongly believes in land filling as the most cost-effective process to dispose solid waste because of land availability and good transportation systems. South and Central America are also dependent on dumps and modern landfills are being developed in some nations such as Argentina, Brazil and Chile.

Australia, with a very large sparsely populated landmass, plentiful supply of fossil fuels and very low energy costs, continues to use its solid wastes for landfilling after recyclable materials have been abstracted. New Zealand is improving its landfills and encourages composting of yard waste.

In Japan, due to lack of available land for landfilling and to reduce the need to import fossil fuel, thermal treatment has been adopted and energy recovery is considered as a recycling activity.

Singapore and Taiwan have also accepted energy recovery from thermal treatment as environmentally beneficial. The economically developing nations such as Korea and Thailand have started developing a regulatory framework for encouraging better solid waste collection and disposal systems. China has also started to look at discards as social and environmental problems.

Experience in a number of Asian countries has shown that simple changes in collection systems, using indigenous, low cost and easily maintainable equipment can provide an improved service to higher proportion of the population. Across the globe, communities and individuals have found creative ways to reduce and manage solid wastes through a coordinated mix of practices that include minimisation of waste at source, recycling and composting or waste combustors.

Solid Waste Management in India

It is estimated that about 1,00,000 MT of municipal solid waste is generated daily in India. Per capita per day waste generation in major cities range from 0.20 kg to 0.60 kg. Generally, the waste collection efficiency ranges between 70 to 90 per cent in metro cities, whereas in several small or medium sized cities, the solid waste collection efficiency is below 50 per cent. It is also estimated that the Urban Local Bodies (ULBs) spend between Rs. 500 to Rs. 1500 per tonne on collection, transportation, treatment and disposal of solid waste. With growth of urban population increase in per capita income, commerce and industry, there has been a rapid expansion in the quantity and composition of solid waste generated in Indian cities. The proper disposal of urban waste is not only necessary for the preservation and improvement of public health but it has an immense potential for resource recovery and urban environment management.

Solid waste management has received attention of late for obvious reasons. Pursuant to the order of the Hon'ble Supreme Court of India dated January 16, 1998 the Ministry of Urban Affairs and Employment, Government of India constituted a committee for identifying the deficiencies in the existing solid waste management systems in India. Three important notifications were issued by Ministry of Environment and Forests, Government of India: (i) Bio-Medical Waste (Management and Handling) Rules, July, 1998 which apply to all persons who generate, collect, receive, store, transport, treat, dispose or handle bio-medical wastes in any form; (ii) Recycled Plastics Manufacture and Usage Rules, 1999 about usage of plastic waste; and (iii) Municipal Solid Wastes (Management and Handling) Rules, September, 2000 which apply to every municipal body responsible for collection, segregation, storage, transportation, processing and disposal of municipal solid waste.

Sources of Waste Generation

Sources of waste generation are: (i) residential premises, (ii) commercial and business establishments, (iii) street sweeping, (iv) institutional premises such as schools, colleges, hotels, restaurants, hospitals, religious places, vegetables, fruit, fish and mutton markets, community and marriage and cinema theatres, etc., (v) trade wastes, (vi) stable/cow dung wastes and (vii) construction and demolition material.

Sources of waste generation in Indian cities can be seen in Table 3.1.

Experience on various aspects of solid waste management reveals that the resource recovery has been emerged as a viable waste disposal strategy. In big cities, waste management, recycling and urban poverty are inextricably linked. Waste recycling depends on a huge network of uneducated urban poor, whose only livelihood is the recovery and reuse of recyclables from solid waste. If properly managed, it could employ around 2 per cent of the urban population.

Table 3.1. Sources of Waste Generation in most of the Indian Cities/Towns

Domestic Waste	Household waste—kitchen, house cleaning, old papers, packing bottles, crockery wares, furnishing materials, garden trimmings, etc.
Commercial Waste	Waste generated at business premises, shops, offices, markets, departmental stores (paper, packing material, spoiled, discarded goods), organic, inorganic, chemically reactive and hazardous waste.
Institutional Waste	Schools, colleges, hospitals, big hotels and restaurants, markets selling vegetables, fruits, flowers, etc., community owned marriage halls, religious places, etc.
Street Sweeping	Unconcerned throwing, littering made by pedestrian traffic, vehicular traffic, stray animals, road side tree leaves, rubbish from drain cleansing, debris, etc.
Industrial/Trade Waste	Manufacturing, processing trade generated waste, etc.
Debris or Construction rejects	Frequent digging of roads by various utilities comprising earth, brick-bats, stones, wooden logs, etc.
Offal Waste	Offal waste generated from slaughter houses, animals, etc., packing institutions and cold storage premises, etc.

It is estimated that these different groups of waste collectors or pickers collect about 5 per cent to 10 per cent of the total solid waste generated in large urban centres and pass it on to the waste recycling sector through various levels of intermediaries. These people adopt different forms: some move from door to door, others pick up the waste from communal waste collection bins on streets and from public places. Large number of poor work on the city garbage dumping sites in appalling sanitary conditions. Also, there are large number of waste recycle workers who work in congested and unhygienic conditions in small informal production and recycling units.

Of late, the municipal officials have started recognising the limitations of technical and managerial solutions to waste management problems, which are rooted in complex socio-cultural and economic aspects. On the face of it, the waste recycling sector, may be far away from the sophisticated, environmentally motivated approach, but the informal network of urban poor performs the task for very different reasons at a fraction of the cost, without any government or municipal support.

Aspects of the dependence of the underprivileged on discharged garbage and role of all these stakeholders are so important for big cities that they deserve to be better understood than they are at present. It is beyond the capacity of most municipal bodies to eliminate these informal network in waste recycling sector. Whatever the innovative alternatives that may be worked out, solid waste management must evolve a positive approach to regard informal waste recovery, reuse and recycling as an integral component of solid waste management in cities and towns.

The waste recovery and recycling return us to the situation of waste recyclers—rag pickers, which are in thousands throughout cities and towns in India. NGOs such as SEWA (Ahmedabad), EXNORA (Chennai), Kashtakari Abhiyan (Pune), Waste Wise (Bengaluru), Apnalaya (Mumbai) and Parisar Vikas (Mumbai) have taken initiative and are involved in waste recycling sector. Some of these initiatives are linked with local colleges or institutions such as SNDT University, Pune, or All India Institute of Local Self Government (AIILSG, Mumbai) which provide technical training and support. These institutions disseminate the knowledge about segregation of waste recycling and enhance the appreciation of the positive contribution made by various groups of waste recyclers in city solid waste management.

However, the extreme unhealthy environment in which all these waste recyclers live and work often in the vicinity of the municipal dumpsites or community waste collection bins, remains a critical problem. Thus, to alleviate the working conditions of these people, their work activity should not be simply treated as informal or nuisance, rather they should be incorporated as useful partners in the cities and towns solid waste management, i.e., segregation of waste, house to house collection prior to final waste disposal and waste recycling.

Partnering with various groups of waste recyclers requires a proper understanding among municipal officials and citizens towards organising rag pickers and waste collectors for house to house waste collection and clean city programme. The rag pickers reduce the burden of local bodies by several million rupees a year in collection, transportation and disposal costs, as well as resultant saving of waste landfill space. This also gives value addition to recyclable waste and help in conserving national resources but their role has not been recognised and acknowledged by the society or the local authorities. Waste pickers can be organised and can get better quality of waste from the doorstep arrangement to give them a better living and much higher dignity of work as waste collector.

The increasing concern during the last decade of both central and state governments and municipal bodies with the clean city programme has firmly placed the solid waste management on the top agenda. The proper disposal of urban solid waste is not only necessary for the preservative and improvement of public health but it has also an immense potential for resource recovery in urban centres.

The Supreme Court of India in its note in writ petition (civil) No. 888/1998 dated, October 4, 2004, has pointed out in the column No. 3 as "Lack of funds is no excuse for inaction. Smaller towns in every state should go and learn from Suryapet in Andhra Pradesh (population 1,03,000) and Namakkal in Tamil Nadu (population 53,000) which have both seen dustbin free 'Zero Garbage Towns' complying with the MSW Rules since 2003 with no financial input from state or central, just good management and a sense of commitment." Thus, Suryapet Municipality stood first in the country to implement Solid Waste (Management and Handling) Rules, 2000. The available information indicates that Suryapet and Namakkal towns have emerged as dustbin free and zero garbage towns. Here, in this chapter, an attempt is made to study how these two towns could achieve the status of zero garbage towns. First, let us concentrate on Suryapet town.

SURYAPET IN ANDHRA PRADESH (A People Participatory Approach)[2]

Suryapet town is the headquarter of revenue division of same name in Nalgonda District (A.P.). It is in Telangana region of Andhra Pradesh state. The town is popularly known as the gateway of Telangana. It is on the National Highway No. 9 at a distance of 132 kms., east of Hyderabad. The river Musi a tributary of river Krishna flows at a distance of 20 kms. Nalgonda railway station on Secunderabad-Nadikudi railway broad gauge line is the nearest rail head at a distance of 50 kms.; from Suryapet town and incidentally, Nalgonda town is also the District headquarters. Historically, it has no significance of worth mentioning. But it was ruled by Chalukyas, Kakatiya and finaliy by Nizam dynasty. Suryapet town contributed several freedom fighters, both against British rule and Nizam rule. Pillamarri village about 5 kms. from the town, is archaeologically famous, three Lord Shiva temples constructed in the village by Kakatiya dynasty.

Suryapet municipality was constituted in the year 1953 as Grade III municipality which was upgraded to Grade II municipality in the year 1984 and to Grade I on November 7, 1998. The area of the town is 23.64 kms. There is a proposal of additional inclusion of an area of about 17.00 kms. in Suryapet municipality. The strength of the council is 31 including 3 co-opted members. There are 28 election wards. As per 2001 census, the town population is 94,660 out of which 49,120 are males and 45,540 are females. The present population of the town is 1,03,000 spreading over 34 sq. kms. The Suryapet municipality is maintaining 241 kms. length of roads and 218 kms. length of drains. The municipality is maintaining sanitation with one sanitary inspector, one health assistant, seven public health jawans and 226 public health workers out of which 98 are male and 128 are female workers. Garbage generated per day is 32.00 MTs. The main economic base of the town is trade and commerce.

Suryapet municipality used to lift the garbage from all dustbins once in a day in the afternoon just like any other municipality. But substantial quantity of garbage used to get accumulated in the dustbins or their surroundings after removal of the garbage. Further, citizens were in the habit of throwing garbage in streets and drains. Due to poor sanitary conditions, most of the people were becoming victims and were affected with various diseases. The conditions prevailing in the slums were worst. Especially, the unhealthy conditions of children started alarming the municipal authorities. After a continuous brainstorming, an idea of zero based solid waste management flashed and started for implementation. Initially, efforts were made to make the town a dustbin free town.

Awareness

The initiative at Suryapet commenced from December, 2002, to make it a dustbin free and zero garbage town. Prior to the beginning of the initiative, all the municipal staff were motivated to do their work sincerely and change their mindset in performing their duties with a strong commitment. Similarly, wide range of awareness programmes were organised involving all stakeholders. All municipal councillors were involved in the implementation of this initiative. First of all, the initiative, started to make aware the sanitary staff about solid waste management. When the initiative was taken to bring reforms in working style, behavioural attitude and liquor habits, the workers exhibited negative attitude. For example, initially workers did not agree to use long stick brooms instead of ordinary brooms. Later, they were convinced. A strong reluctance was faced while conducting awareness in poor clusters due to their ignorance, illiteracy, etc. Awareness programmes were conducted by officials, doctors, school children, women households, etc. Before starting the new scheme, dustbins were removed from the entire town, as the garbage was to be collected directly from households.

Situation before the Initiative began

The initiative of keeping the Suryapet municipality free from dustbins and garbage began in the month of January, 2003. The situation before the initiative was as follows:

- The garbage from households and commercial establishments used to be deposited in and around dustbins.
- The garbage was used to be dumped at lowlying areas.
- Municipal vehicles used to lift the garbage once in the morning, but substantial quantity of garbage used to get accumulated in the dustbins after lifting.

- People were accustomed to throw garbage in the drains and streets indiscriminately.
- There was low public health awareness and lack of civic sense among citizens.
- Lack of responsibility among municipal staff to keep the town clean.
- The net result was inefficient garbage collection and disposal giving an ugly and unhygienic appearance in all parts of the town.
- The weaker sections of the community and children were most affected due to poor insanitary conditions in the town.

Organising Awareness Programmes

A wide range of awareness programmes were organised in the town involving DWCUA groups about the necessity of keeping the city clean. Similar programmes were conducted in 64 schools and 18 colleges creating awareness among students about the necessity of keeping all streets in a clean manner. Awareness meetings were conducted among owners and workers of commercial establishments about their role with regard to keep the town clean. Awareness programmes were also conducted for household women, doctors and officials and owners of hotels, marriage halls, non-veg stalls through interactions, speeches, slide shows, etc.

Motivation of Public Health Staff

Training programmes were conducted to motivate public health staff to do their work sincerely and to change their mind-set in performing their duties in a committed manner. Meditation and yoga classes were conducted for public health staff to bring a change in their attitude and to inculcate a sense of responsibility to perform their duties properly.

Formulation of Strategies

- To keep the town clean without dustbins and zero garbage, it was proposed to collect garbage from house to house in municipal tractors by the public health workers. All residents were supplied with two plastic bins to deposit wet garbage in green colour bin and dry garbage in red colour bin duly segregating the garbage at source. The residents would hand over the bins whenever the vehicle visited their streets and houses.

- To clean the streets and drains regularly, daily cleaning of streets and drains was planned to keep the town clean and tidy.

Present Practices

- Entire public health staff is deployed in convenient batches for collection of garbage door to door in a vehicle, cleaning of roads and drains. Entire municipal area is divided into 7 zones and each zone allotted with a vehicle and required staff.
- Levy of a penalty of Rs. 100 on all persons who throw garbage in streets and drains. This is intended to act as a deterrent against persons who throw garbage in drains and streets.

Mobilisation of Resources

Maintenance of sanitation is one of the statutory functions of the municipality. An amount of Rs. 124.00 lakhs was utilised during the year 2002-03 for this purpose. One Sanitary Inspector, one Health Assistant, seven Public Health Jawans and 227 Public Health Workers are employed for the maintenance of sanitation. Nine tractors, three motored tri cycles and three cycle-rickshaws are deployed for this purpose. The Municipal Commissioner and Municipal Council are responsible for implementation of the initiative.

Process

- The entire municipal area is divided into seven territorial zones allocating required public health staff, vehicles and equipment for maintenance of sanitation.
- Micro level plan was prepared for implementation of the initiative in all the seven zones duly taking into consideration number of households, length of roads and drains in each zone.

- Two coloured plastic bins are supplied to all residents free of cost to deposit wet garbage in green bin and dry garbage in red bin by segregating garbage at source.
- Municipal vehicles with public health staff are sent to all streets daily to collect garbage directly from the residents. As soon as the vehicle reaches a house, the driver blows a whistle to indicate the arrival of the vehicle. Immediately, the residents handover the bins to public health staff who will put the garbage in the vehicle. Dry garbage is deposited in a separate receptacle.
- The garbage generated after sweeping the streets is also deposited in the vehicle when it comes for collection of garbage from door to door.
- All dustbins in the town have been removed as garbage is collected directly from all household and commercial establishments, daily.
- Regular cleaning of all drains is undertaken, and the silt collected therefrom is removed daily.
- Separate vehicle is deployed to collect bulk garbage from hospitals, hotels and restaurants, mutton and chicken stalls at different timings.
- Separate vehicle is deployed from 10 a.m. daily to collect garbage door to door from all shops situated on main roads.
- Separate vehicle is deployed once in a week to lift debris from all parts of the town.
- The wet garbage is transported to compost yard for producing vermin compost. A separate municipal land is used for this purpose.
- The dry garbage is further segregated into paper, plastic, glass and metal, and sold out to scrap dealers.
- The daily reports of public health subordinates are monitored by Municipal Commissioner to identify problems and to initiate remedial action.

Problems faced in Implementation

- Reluctance of public health staff in the initial stages in the implementation of the initiative due to close monitoring.
- Continued throwing of garbage on the streets and drains in the initial stages of implementation on account of previous habits.

Results Achieved

- The initiative taken by the municipality has brought a remarkable visible change in the appearance of the town.
- 100 per cent door to door collection of garbage without any additional staff and machinery.
- Quality of life has been improved in the city especially in slum areas.
- Spreaded the concept and practices of converting the waste to wealth.
- Healthy environment has been created in the town.
- 100 per cent source segregation through two bin systems.
- Citizens are not throwing garbage in streets and drains.
- Special arrangements for depositing garbage by the footpath dwellers was tackled by providing bins to each electrical pole at a distance of 60 metres.
- 100 per cent of the roads and drains are cleaned everyday.
- Before the commencement of the initiative in January, 2003, fifty per cent of the garbage was lifted whereas 100 per cent of garbage is being lifted after initiative.
- 360 community dustbins are completely removed from all parts of the town providing a neat appearance of roads and streets in the town.
- 52,000 bins (green and red) distributed to 26,000 families at free of cost.
- Revenue generation through the sale of recyclable and compost is Rs. 80,000 per month.
- The silt and debris is dumped in lowlying areas.

- Strict action was initiated against the owners of commercial establishments who throw garbage in streets and drains by levying a penalty of Rs. 100 for each offence. This has yielded good results and the percentage of people throwing garbage on roads and drains has come to about zero.
- The initiative was discussed in detail in the meetings of Municipal Council and their approval was obtained.

Peoples' Participation

- Public awareness was created through public announcement, distribution of pamphlets, and through street plays and songs.
- Meetings were conducted in early mornings at street corners explaining the necessity of keeping the town clean and the problems created due to throwing of garbage on roads and in drains creating unsanitary conditions in the streets resulting in communicable diseases.
- In street corner meetings, residents were asked to segregate the garbage into wet and dry in the household itself and put into separate plastic bins supplied by the municipality.
- Further, the residents were requested to hand over the garbage bins to the public health workers as and when municipal vehicles visited their street and blew the whistle in front of their house.
- Meetings were conducted with different professional and trade groups to follow the new process.
- Meetings were conducted with NGOs, cable TV and media to extend their cooperation in the implementation of the initiative.

Monitoring

- In the beginning of the implementation of the initiative, each zone was placed under the supervision of one officer for close monitoring.
- Daily reports are submitted by public health subordinates regarding cleaning of all streets and drains and collection

of garbage door to door from all households and other establishments.

Impact

- Without the involvement of private initiatives/NGOs, Suryapet municipality has implemented this project on its own.
- Citizens are quite satisfied with this initiative and this has resulted in vast improvement in collection of taxes.
- There is considerable fall in the occurrence of communicable diseases.
- Employment and enterprise opportunities in Green Industry have been created.
- Documented all the activities of the project for further guidance and replication.
- The citizens are very happy and quite satisfied with the performance of the municipality.
- The overall image of the Municipal Council has gone up high in the galaxy of services provided to the citizens and in the cleanliness of the town.

Income Generation through Recycling of Garbage

The segregated garbage (organic and inorganic) from the residents, shopkeepers and other garbage generators was collected separately at collection point itself and the inorganic waste is further segregated in the plant constructed exclusively for the purpose and sold out locally. The organic waste is directly formed into beds and moisture is maintained by spraying water mixed with cow dung and such beds are maintained till these are decomposed into a maximum of 50 per cent and then the worms will be left into these beds. The wet garbage has been converted into vermi composting.

Initially, the Zero Waste Management (ZWM) project was planned to generate income out of the garbage (15,000 tonnes per day) collected from the town. Accordingly, this practice had given a low income initially, and the income increased by the end of 2003 to the tune of Rs. 1000 per day. At present, the income through recyclables and processed compost is Rs. 2000 per day.

However, according to the municipal officials, as on date the municipality is getting Rs. 80,000 income per month.

Lessons Learnt

- Micro level planning, motivation of staff and public participation can give exemplary results.
- Involvement of Municipal Councillors in the implementation of the initiative is essentially required to make the project success.
- The organic wastes can be used either for power plant or for composting activity in a befitting manner, if the separation is done at source level perfectly.
- Daily monitoring by Municipal Commissioner is required to implement the initiative successfully.
- Healthy environment can be made possible.
- Enforcement of levying fine of Rs. 100 on commercial establishments for throwing garbage in streets and drains is equally responsible for the success of the initiative.
- Incidence of communicable diseases can definitely be checked.
- Creation of awareness among citizens, all associations, institutions, NGOs, CBOs and Media is essential for proper implementation of the initiative.
- Inorganic wastes can be recycled through which income can be generated.

Transferability

- This initiative can be replicated in all municipalities with a population of less than one lakh without any difficulty as effective supervision in small and medium type municipalities by municipal commissioner is feasible. As maintenance of sanitation is one of the key functions of the ULBs, this practice can be implemented with the available resources—financial, technical and human. The initiative can be easily implemented in smaller and medium municipalities as the process involves only change in the manner of collecting garbage from house to house instead of from dustbins.

Sustainability

- The entire population is aware of the initiative and highly appreciative of the new process.
- The citizens are in favour of continuing the initiative as garbage is removed daily from their houses without accumulation at no extra cost.
- The public health staff is satisfied with this initiative as physical handling of garbage is avoided. Further, the strenuous nature of lifting garbage from dustbins is completely eliminated as garbage is collected only from the households directly, that too daily.
- The initiative is implemented without any additional finances.
- The Municipal Council is extending full support to the initiative.
- Modern equipment for transporting garbage generated from sweeping of roads has to be provided instead of traditional wheel barrow to ensure more turnovers from public health workers and to make the programme sustainable.

It may be mentioned that Suryapet Municipality implemented the strategy of Solid Waste Management prior to the framing of Municipal Solid Wastes (Management and Handling) Rules, 2000. Thus, Suryapet Municipality has fulfilled Supreme Court ruling for safeguarding the environmental and health factors of the people. Suryapet Municipality has proved that there is no need of landfilling and the Zero Waste Management is possible without extra effort, expenditure, manpower, and with the economical and environmental friendly system. Zero waste management produces excellent substitution for virgin raw materials and consequentially avoids resource depletion. Further, it leads to waste minimisation thereby saving a tremendous chunk of valuable urban land, which otherwise may be used for landfilling.

Through this successful project, not only other urban local bodies but also other agencies learn the process of planning, designing, mobilising, implementing, monitoring and evaluating successful Zero Waste Management (ZWM) programme of a city/town and the resources and methodologies to carry the plan completion.

Comparison on Implementation of Initiative

Garbage Collection

Sl. No.	Particulars	Before	After
1.	Average quantity of waste generated per day @ 0.200 kgs. per capita	-	18.00 Tonnes
2.	Shops and Establishments	-	1.50 Tonnes
3.	Vegetable Market	50.00 Tonnes	2.50 Tonnes
4.	Hospital and Chicken waste	-	5.30 Tonnes
5.	Debris (Building Material)	-	7.50 Tonnes
6.	Drainage Silt	-	5.00 Tonnes
	Total:	50.00 Tonnes	39.80 Tonnes

Comparison on Implementation of Initiative System Adopted

Sl. No.	Particulars	Before	After
1.	No. of Community Dustbins	360	-Nil-
2.	System of Collection	Community Dustbins	Door to door collection duly segregated at source

Comparison on Implementation of Initiative:

Revenue Generation

Sl. No.	Particulars	Before	After
1.	Composting of organic waste	-	60%
2.	Recyclable waste (Due to lack of infrastructural facilities the total organic waste could not processed)	-	90%

Comparison on Implementation of Initiative:

Machinery

S. No.	Particulars	Before	After
1.	No. of Tractors	9	10
2.	No. of Workers	217	227

Segregation of Wet and Dry Garbage in Baskets

Green basket (Wet garbage)	Red basket (Dry garbage)
WASTES MEANT FOR GREEN BASKET	WASTES MEANT FOR RED BASKET
Vegetables wastes	Papers, Plastic covers
Coconut	All types of polythene covers
Non-vegetarian wastes	Dry flowers
Lizards	Wooden things, Napkins
Cockroaches	Bottles, waste clothes
Ash, charcoal	Old chappals
Fruits peel	Mineral water bottles
Broom	Electric wires
Coffee dust	Chocolate papers
Garden wastes	Leather items
Coir, hair	Powerless batteries
Egg shell	Unwantod notebooks
Kitchen waste	Fused bulbs, boxes
Banana leaves	Rubber items
Tea dust	Empty paste tubes
	Empty power boxes
	Medicines, waste plastic, etc.

Public Health Workers

Detail of Zones	Male	Female	Total
Zone-1	17	18	35
Zone-2	17	15	32
Zone-3	15	17	32
Zone-4	14	15	29
Zone-5	10	21	31
Zone-6	11	20	31
Zone-7	14	22	36
Total	**98**	**128**	**226**

Recycle Waste Price List

Sl. No.	Product	Weight	Rate (Rs.)
1.	Iron	Kg	10.00
2.	Sheet	Kg	9.00
3.	Aluminium	Kg	40.00
4.	Brass	Kg	80.00
5.	Bronze	Kg	110.00
6.	Stainless Steel	Kg	15.00
7.	Plastic	Kg	10.00
8.	Plastic Chappals	Kg	7.00
9.	Plastic Tea Cups	Kg	4.00
10.	Note Paper	Kg	7.00
11.	School Book	Kg	3.00
12.	Newspaper	Kg	4.00
13.	Mica Cover (smooth)	Kg	5.00
14.	Beer Bottle (new)	Piece	4.00
15.	Beer Bottle (old)	Piece	4.00
16.	Quarter Bottle	Piece	1.25
17.	Milk Cover	Kg	10.00
18.	Oil Cover	Kg	6.00
19.	White Records	Kg	6.00
20.	Glass	Kg	1.00
21.	Glass (ordinary)	Piece	0.75
22.	PVC	Kg	20.00
23.	Soda Bottle	Piece	1.00
24.	Beer Bottle (small)	Piece	0.50
25.	Newspaper (waste)	Kg	2.50
26.	Royal Apple Bottle	Piece	0.50
27.	Bottle (pound)	Piece	0.50
28.	X-Rat Paper	Kg	20.00

Work Schedule

Daily working hours

5.00 a.m.	: Attendance
5.15 a.m. to 10.00 a.m.	: Door to Door collection of segregated garbage at source.
(8.00 a.m. to 8.30 a.m.)	: Tea Break
10.00 a.m. to 12.00 Noon	: (1) Collection of segregated garbage from shops and business establishments. (2) Collection of segregated Hospital waste.
2.00 p.m. to 5.00 p.m.	: (1) Lifting of Drainage silt. (2) Collection of non-vegetarian waste from Chicken and Mutton stalls.

Note: Due to shortage of vehicles shift system is arranged wherever necessary.

General Information

1. Number of persons involved in door to door garbage collection zone-wise:

(a)	Zone I	Number of families 5,950	35 members per day
(b)	Zone II	Number of families 4,050	32 members per day
(c)	Zone III	Number of families 4,900	32 members per day
(d)	Zone IV	Number of families 5,700	29 members per day
(e)	Zone V	Number of families 2,750	31 members per day
(f)	Zone VI	Number of families 5,100	31 members per day
(g)	Zone VII	Number of families 3,300	36 members per day

Notes:

1. The door to door collection of garbage by source segregation is done at free of cost.
2. Night sanitation on main roads of commercial areas are being done with 12 workers.

Training

Training has been provided to public health workers and supervisory staff in the following subjects:

- Maintenance of discipline.
- Behavioural attitude.
- Keeping good health.
- Discarding of bad habits, i.e., smoking, liquor, playing cards, illegal sexual contacts, etc.
- Maintenance of courtesies during the working hours and also with the households.
- Free health check-up camps to PH centres periodically.

Composting Yard: Infrastructure

1. Composting shed (thatched) of 60 × 30 for culture.
2. Composting beds under thatched roof in an area of 120 × 80 mtrs.
3. Composting beds (200 × 400 mtrs.) under shelters provided with leaves with thatched roof.
4. Bore with motor provided.
5. A shed (pucca) for further segregation of dry garbage and storage of dry garbage bundles.
6. Electrical supply connection with lighting facilities.

Distribution of Dustbins—Wardwise Details

Sl. No.	Wards	No. of Families	No. of Dustbins Distributed	No. of Tractors Engaged in each zone
1.	Ward No. 1	1,520	3,040	1 Tractor
2.	Ward No. 2	1,650	3,300	
3.	Ward No. 3	940	1,880	
4.	Ward No. 4	1,100	2,200	
5.	Ward No. 5	850	1,700	1 Tractor
6.	Ward No. 6	940	1,880	
7.	Ward No. 7	950	1,900	
8.	Ward No. 8	1,350	2,700	
9.	Ward No. 9	950	1,900	1 Tractor
10.	Ward No. 10	850	1,700	
11.	Ward No. 11	1,740	3,480	
12.	Ward No. 12	1,460	2,920	
13.	Ward No. 13	1,200	2,400	1 Tractor
14.	Ward No. 14	1,300	2,600	
15.	Ward No. 15	1,250	2,500	
16.	Ward No. 16	950	1,900	
17.	Ward No. 17	650	1,300	
18.	Ward No. 18	550	1,100	1 Tractor
19.	Ward No. 19	550	1,100	
20.	Ward No. 20	1,040	2,080	
21.	Ward No. 21	950	1,900	1 Tractor
22.	Ward No. 22	1,040	2,080	
23.	Ward No. 23	1,050	2,100	
24.	Ward No. 24	1,050	2,100	
25.	Ward No. 25	970	1,940	1 Tractor
26.	Ward No. 26	1,150	2,300	
27.	Ward No. 27	1,050	2,100	
28.	Ward No. 28	1,100	2,200	

Note: One Tractor is engaged exclusively for main roads.

Appreciation and Awards

- The initiative of dustbin free and zero garbage Suryapet has been appreciated and selected as good practice by the United Nations Habitat and United Nations Human Settlements Programmes, by Central Institute of Plastic

Engineering and Technology, Hyderabad, during the one day conference held in the month of March, 2004, four-day seminar conducted by M/s Toxic Links at Delhi during the month of April, 2004.

- Many articles appreciating the effort and identifying Suryapet Urban Local Body as only urban town which has implemented SWM Rules, 2000 in a perfect manner in India, have been published in various newspapers and journals.
- The Hon'ble Supreme Court of India in its record of proceedings in Writ Petition (Civil) No. 888/1998 filed by Mrs. Almitra H. Patel and another, have noted that "lack of funds is no excuse for inaction. Smaller towns in every state should go and learn from Suryapet in Andhra Pradesh and Namakkal in Tamil Nadu, which have both seen dustbin free zero garbage towns complying with MSW Rules since 2003, with no financial input from State or Centre, just good management and a sense of commitment."

NAMAKKAL IN TAMIL NADU (A Public Privatisation Model)[3]

Namakkal Municipality was established on January 17, 1970 as class III and upgraded as class II on February 14, 1988. According to 2001 census, the town population is 53,041 and the area has been spread over to 10.24 sq. kms. There are 30 municipal wards in the town. The Solid Waste Management team of Namakkal municipality comprises of 3 sanitary inspectors 9 sanitary supervisors, one field assistant and 146 sanitary workers. For solid waste management, 2 mini tipper lorries, 4 mini lorries, one sullage lorry, 90 handpush carts, 252 drums for push carts are functioning. In Namakkal Municipality, garbage is supposed to be collected from 14,891 residential houses, one daily market, one Ulavar market, one weekly market, 52 hotels, one slaughter house and 2,630 commercial buildings.

The vision of the Urban Local Body to make Namakkal a Zero Garbage Town by 2003 was the motivation behind the initiative. It was intended to design a long-term and sustainable strategy by involving citizens and other stakeholders in the 'Zero Garbage Drive'. Under this scheme, the following responsibilities were privatised. Namakkal is the first municipality in the country to privatise all components in solid waste management.

- Door to door collection of waste with segregation at source.
- Manufacturing of vermi compost from organic waste.
- Sale of recyclable from organic waste.
- Transportation and disposal of inorganic waste.

In Namakkal Municipality, contractor provides service to 75 per cent of town's area and municipality manages the remaining 25 per cent area. Similarly, municipality handles 75 per cent of waste and contractor handles 25 per cent of waste. Out of a total of 192 conservancy staff, 122 are municipal employees and 70 are private employees.

Municipal Solid Wastes (Management and Handling) Rules, 2000
SCHEDULE
Status in Namakkal Town

Sl. No.	Activities to be done	Time Limit	Action
1.	Setting up of waste processing and disposal facilities	Dec. 31, 2003 or before	Implemented
2.	Monitoring the performance of waste processing and disposal facilities	Once in six months	Implemented
3.	Improvement of existing landfill sites as per provisions of these rules	Dec. 31, 2003 or before	Not yet. Support needed
4.	Identification of landfill sites for future use and making site(s) ready for operation	Dec. 31, 2003 or before	Implemented

The Activities to be Completed as per Solid Waste Management Handling Rules, 2000

- Garbage should not be burnt.
- Door to door collection of garbage to be done.
- Garbages to be removed from slum areas and hotels, restaurants, office premises, commercial complexes, etc.

- Hospital wastes should not be mixed with other garbages.
- Building materials should not be mixed with other wastes.
- Wandering animals should not be permitted near the garbage.
- Segregation of wastes at source, i.e., the producers of wastes.
- Vermi compost to be manufactured from organic waste.
- Inorganic wastes to be buried.

Problem from the Daily Generating Wastes

Namakkal municipality faced lot of problems because of the generation of wastes like (a) foul smell, (b) uncleaned situation, (c) communicable diseases, (d) preventing the smooth flow in drains, whereby flies and mosquitoes breeding, (e) spreading of diseases from pigs and flies, (f) deficiency in soil fertility, and (g) environmental pollution, etc.

Benefits of Door to Door Collection with Segregation at Source

- Implementation of Municipal Solid Waste Handling Rules, 2000.
- Appreciation from public for good services.
- People themselves practised segregation of wastes.
- Primary segregation of organic and inorganic waste.
- 100 per cent removal of garbage.
- All uncovered areas are being covered.
- Effective delivery of public health activities.
- A stage has come that people should not throw wastes on streets and roads, etc.
- Competition between private and municipality to show their efficiency.
- To deliver good services.
- Garbage free streets and roads.
- Removal of dustbins from entire town (dustbin free town).

- Manufacturing of vermi compost from organic waste. By achieving these activities the unreachable goal has come into reality in reaching Zero Garbage Level.

10 Points Charter to Achieve Zero Garbage Town

1. To extend the scheme of door to door collection with segregation of the entire town and make the streets and roads without garbage.
2. Introduction of night sweeping at bus stand and important roads, etc. and maintain cleanliness round the clock.
3. To extend the schemes of door to door collection and sweeping on holidays and Sundays and make the town clean on all days.
4. Make the parks and burial grounds beautiful and attractive through NGOs and voluntary agencies.
5. Removal of the encroachments from all roads and streets and maintain the same by preventing them from re-encroachments.
6. To prevent the roadside and maintain it beautifully by planning trees.
7. Removal of pigs and dogs away from the town.
8. Levy service charges on the hotels, kalyana mandapams, commercial complexes and garbage generating industries.
9. Manufacturing of vermi compost from organic waste through voluntary organisation/private bodies and sell the inorganic recycling garbage.
10. Engaging two mob-up teams with two auto model carriers to remove the waste then and there round the clock and make the town free of garbage.

By implementing all the above tasks, Namakkal town has emerged as free from garbage and was announced no Garbage Town from July 1, 2003.

Steps Undertaken in Solid Waste Management

- Privatisation of door to door collection with segregation at source into organic and inorganic wastes.

- Privatisation of manufacturing vermi compost from organic waste on BOT basis.
- Secondary collection of inorganic waste into recyclable waste and inorganic waste.
- Sale of recyclable wastes.
- Burial of inorganic non-recyclable wastes.
- Converting compost yard into a beautiful garden.

Compost Yard

Presently compost yard is located at a distance of 2 kms. from the town in an area of 8.53 acres. The Namakkal Municipality is getting additional income from the compost yard as stated below:

1. **Sale of Vermi Compost**

   Sale of vermi compost—one M.T. is Rs. 325

   Annual Income = 325 × 2 × 30 × 12 = Rs. 3,34,000

2. **Sale of Recyclable Waste**

   Sale of recyclable waste—one M.T. is Rs. 50

   Annual Income = 50 × 2 × 30 × 12 = Rs. 36,000

   Total: 3,34,000 + 36,000 = Rs. 3,70,000

Environmental Improvement Measures: Special Features

- Night sweeping.
- Sweeping on all holidays and Sundays.
- Exhibiting the slogans on all hoardings, autos, rickshaws, wall writings, etc.
- Utilising the services of the women neighbourhood committee.
- Frequent press meets.
- 100 per cent removal of dustbin.
- Planting of trees on streets and roads.
- Removal of entire dogs and pigs.
- Removal of encroachments on roads and streets.
- Making of the streets and roads garbage free.

- Free flow of drains without stagnation.
- Converting the compost yard into a beautiful garden.

Since the door to door collection is being done by private bodies, 14 sweepers have been engaged for night sweeping on main roads and bus stands so as to make the town clean round the clock. Sweeping and door to door collection is being done on all Sundays and holidays to make the town clean on all days.

Mob-up Van with Public Address System

Two auto model carriers have been purchased and put into use as a mob-up van to pick up the wastes which fall on streets and they have been used with public address system to educate the public about the zero garbage system. Two sanitary inspectors have been appointed for this purpose and also to impose spot fine upon the people who throw the wastes on streets and roads. This model is more successful in declaring the town as a 'Zero Garbage' one.

With the involvement of private parties and people being mobilised for keeping their city clean, the municipality is now able to provide a better level of service. There is a considerable improvement in apparent environment in the town. 'Information and Education Campaign (IEC)' and peoples' support and their active participation are the secrets behind the success of the 'Zero Garbage Town'.

Appreciation and Awards

- Thiru K. Rajendram, IAS, District Collector, Namakkal has honoured with a shield for the efforts taken by the Namakkal Municipal Council and Commissioner to reach the Zero Garbage Level.
- The Commissioner of Municipal Administration, Govt. of Tamil Nadu also visited the town and categorically declared that Namakkal town was fit for declaring Zero Garbage Town.
- Dr. A.K. Saxena, Group Head (Env. and Mgt.) National Productivity Council, New Delhi visited Namakkal town on September 3, 2003 and has congratulated the Municipal Council and Municipal Commissioner for reaching to the stage of 'Zero Garbage Town'.

Thus, it may be included that recognitions of the work done through honours and awards play a useful role to motivate people. The Hon'ble Supreme Court has rightly emphasised that it is not the lack of resources which is responsible for the prevailing unhygienic conditions in the urban areas, it is rather due to the lack of will on the part of people and administration.

GREATER VISAKHAPATNAM MUNICIPAL CORPORATION IN ANDHRA PRADESH (PRIVATISATION MODEL)

Greater Visakhapatnam Municipal Corporation in Andhra Pradesh generates as much as 750 m. tonnes of wastes per annum. The Visakhapatnam has leased in 100 acres of land for 20 years for the final disposal of urban wastes.

Best is the disposal of bio-medical wastes which has become an acute problem and is creating health hazards in most of the urban centres. The system evolved has many social benefits (externalities) like reducing the carbon credit and greenhouse gases. This also reduces the adverse effect on Ozone layer.

In the Bio-Medical Waste Plant first recyclable wastes like needles, plastics, etc. are separated, then rest is burnt at high temperature. The smoke is passed through a chimney at a very great height so that there is no adverse effect on the city environment. A very small component of ash left is then used for landfilling and usually bought by landfilling firms. It may be mentioned here that in Punjab for the important Municipal Corporations of Ludhiana, Amritsar, Jalandhar and Patiala, the disposal of bio-medical wastes has become a major bone of contention between the Punjab Pollution Control Board and the Hospital authorities. The municipal corporations should charge a nominal fee from the government hospitals and commercial fees from the private commercial hospitals, failing which they should be fined.

Cleanliness of the City

Cleanliness of the city is done throughout the day. The workers (safai karamcharies) remain on the job throughout the day and even during the night, particularly alongside the beach road. So that when visitors or tourists come in the morning, the total environment is clean and healthy. Drains are also cleaned daily and the floating material or garbage is separated and put in the garbage carriers.

Even the worst affected areas like slums and vegetable market are also daily cleaned around the clock. Slum dwellers were found to be enjoying the facilities of safe drinking water, common toilets, clean drains, etc. The most unhygienic place usually found in modern cities is vegetable market. Even this place was found to be well maintained. And even shopkeepers were seen engaged in removing the roughage and vegetable wastes. The municipal corporation not only endeavours to maintain the cleanliness through private contracts, but also levies fines on the defaulters.

From the households wheel barrows/rickshaw-rehris (pushcarts) collect the wastes and garbage at very nominal rate of Rs. 10 per month and put in big containers called dustbins (total no. is 650), which have been located at very convenient and strategic points. The nearby residents and the commercial establishments can directly put their garbage in these containers. The rag pickers or wheel barrow carriers are often seen segregating the recyclable or reusable material. The dustbins or containers with garbage are carried by the dumpy placers (39 are owned by the corporation and 45 are hired @ of Rs. 650 per day). These are then weighed in the city garbage centre and unloaded in big trucks which are carried to the final disposal point, which is located 20 kms. away from the town on Chennai-Kolkata road on 100 acres of land leased for 20 years for the final disposal of urban wastes. The final disposal point again is maintained and looked after by the sanitary inspector. Also the Senior Medical Officer or Chief Medical Officer often pay visit to the final disposable point. Here again the ragpickers collect the recyclable material and the rest is burnt. In fact, the urban wastes which is ultimately burnt has great potentials to generate electricity. The private parties are reported to provide it @ Rs. 4.0 per unit. But the State Electricity Board declined the move as it would be uneconomical in the sense that the power is otherwise available @ Rs. 2.0 per unit. But considering the total social benefits in terms of its positive effect on environment and ecology, the authorities should not compare only commercial costs and commercial benefits but also social costs and social benefits. Many of the government activities would fail on the former front but succeed on the latter front, i.e., total net social benefits may exceed the total commercial costs. Since the state governments in India lack resources, therefore, the centre should come forward in a big way to tackle the problem of urban waste management.

SCHEME OF MAIN ROAD SANITATION, GREATER VISAKHAPATNAM MUNICIPAL CORPORATION, VISAKHAPATNAM

Greater Visakhapatnam Municipal Corporation of Visakhapatnam introduced, Main Road sanitation scheme and aims at involving the citizens in their respective areas for effective monitoring and day-to-day supervision in all the related activities of the proposed works. The works are purely temporary in nature and the societies proposed to be selected for execution of works are free to carry out the works by engaging men or equipment and machines subject to the condition that those proposed to be selected shall themselves be personally present in the respective areas allotted to them for carrying out the works. No benamees and proxies shall be allowed on their behalf. Cases of such nature will be severely dealt with by cancellation of work, forfeiture of the security deposits and blacklisting of such societies by debarring them from works programme of any department under Municipal Corporation of Visakhapatnam.

The Scheme for Main Road Sanitation (Night Work)

The work package consists of cleaning unit.

Cleaning Unit

A total road length of 4 kms. of main roads makes one cleaning unit. The roads, footpaths, table drains, central media, road dividers and open places on the roadside are part of the cleaning unit.

Nature of Work

- Removal of litters, plastic rubbles and other wastes.
- Scraping of road silt and sand and removal of the same from the entire road, dividers, road margins, etc.

- Surface cleaning of the entire road stretch including footpaths, road margins, etc.
- Removal of posters and wall writings from notified sites.
- Removal of heaps of debris on the roads, footpaths and garbage collected shall be deposited in the iron bins available nearby.
- Attending to water stagnation points due to rains, etc. on the roads.
- Mopping up of work by litter collecting, scrapping and collection of sand and silt and removal from footpaths and road margins in the following forenoon (list not exhaustive).
- Sprinkling of disinfectant mixture of bleaching powder+lime at these points after lifting the garbage.

Timings

10 p.m. to 5 a.m. (in the main cleaning work)

7 a.m. to 12 noon and 3 p.m. to 6 p.m. (Mopping operation and maintaining litter free roads)

Work Norms and Conditions for Night Shift

- The societies shall have to furnish a detailed cleaning plan for the main cleaning operation in the night and for mopping up operation in the day separately.
- The work shall be carried out on all the days including Sundays and public holidays.
- Attendance points should be fixed separately as:

	Night Shift	Day Shift
Reporting attendance point(s)	11 p.m.,	7 a.m. and 3 p.m.
Departure attendance point(s)	5 a.m.,	12 noon and 6 p.m.

- A full time supervisor for each unit for both night and day mop up separately has to be engaged by the societies. He shall be available in the uniform clothes for easy identification by the inspecting officers.
- The societies (supervisors) should be personally present in the field for both night and day mop up with wireless

sets to ensure completion of work satisfactorily. The agency should carry a photo identity card (for easy identification by the inspecting officers) at the work site.

- The societies should furnish daily progress report to the authorised officer of the VMC on the performance.

Works Norms and Conditions for Day Shifts

- The societies shall prepare and furnish a detailed cleaning plan for the first shift and second shift for each cleaning unit in the work area immediately after selection and before the allotment of work order.
- The work shall be carried out on all the days including Sundays and public holidays.
- Attendance points should be fixed for verifying attendance at 7 a.m. and 12 noon for first shift, and 3 p.m. and 6 p.m. for the second shift.
- A full time supervisor for each cleaning unit has to be engaged and shall be physically present at the work site in uniform clothes (for easy identification) from 7 a.m. to 12 noon and 3 p.m. to 6 p.m. everyday.
- The societies shall be personally present at the work site everyday from 7 a.m. to 12 noon and 3 p.m. to 6 p.m. along with cell phone and execute the work.
- No benamees and proxies will be allowed. The societies should also keep a photo identify card (for easy identification by the inspecting officer).
- The societies should submit daily progress report to the authorised officer of the VMC in the prescribed format after satisfactory completion of the work.
- The societies shall be prepared to accept additional responsibilities for attending the emergencies as directed by the VMC in keeping the area clean.
- Tools and equipment will be supplied by VMC.

Security Deposit towards Performance Guarantee

The security deposit amount of Rs. 25,000 shall be paid through demand draft drawn on any scheduled commercial bank in favour of the Commissioner, Municipal Corporation of

Visakhapatnam, at the time of finalisation of tenders and after the work is allotted. Cheques will not be accepted.

The security deposits of the contractors held by the VMC under the existing work package cannot be considered as security deposits for the new package.

The payment of wages to the workers employed by the contractors shall be by way of cheque/demand draft and in accordance with the rates notified by the District Collector. A certificate that the wages have been paid in accordance with the said notification along with xerox copies of DD/Cheques should invariably be furnished by the contractor every month to VMC.

Fines Regime

Since the work is of very important nature for keeping the city clean and protect the health of the citizens, a detailed fines regime is introduced by the VMC for regulating the works. The Agency if fails to carryout the work as per the norms and their recurrence may lead to termination of the contract and forfeiture of the performance guarantee deposits.

GREATER VISAKHAPATNAM MUNICIPAL CORPORATION

Part-1: Definitions

All the 'terms', 'words' and phrases defined and used in the context in HMC Act, 1955, shall apply and shall be understood in the same context.

In considering these terms and conditions and specifications, the following expressions shall have meaning herein assigned to them unless there is something in the subject or context in consistent with such meaning in the HMC Act, 1955.

'Contractor' shall mean the societies satisfying the following conditions as per G.O.Ms. No. 581 MA, dated Nov. 6, 1996.

1. The societies should be registered under societies registration Act.
2. The members should belong to Retd. PH Workers/ their children/and other SC/ST community people having experience of sanitation work such as badli workers.

3. The society with registration proof/evidence has to produce that all the workers in the society have worked as badli in Greater Visakhapatnam, Greater Visakhapatnam Municipal Corporation and in case of SC/ST workers, caste certificate from MRO, Vsp., shall be produced.

Experience of sanitation work such as badli workers whose tender has been accepted by the appropriate authority with the said corporation and who has entered into an agreement with the said corporation for fulfillment of the contract, shall include the legal representatives/successors and assigns of the tenderer.

'Health Officer' means the Chief Medical Officer of Health or such other officer on whom powers are vested to act as the health officer for the purpose of the contract.

'Association' means the societies registered under the societies registration Act for the purpose of proper sanitation maintenance for the purpose of proper execution of the contract by the Commissioner.

As per the G.O.Ms. No. 581/MA, dated Nov. 6, 1996 the societies should be registered under societies registration Act.

The members should belong to retired Public Health Workers, their children/and other scheduled caste/scheduled tribe community people having experience of sanitation work such as badli worker. 'Commissioner' means the commissioner of the Greater Visakhapatnam, Greater Visakhapatnam Municipal Corporation, Visakhapatnam and includes such other officers on whom the powers by the Commissioner has vested specifically for the purpose of the contract.

Wherever Commissioner is named as a final authority for any decision shall mean only the Commissioner of the Greater Visakhapatnam, Greater Visakhapatnam Municipal Corporation, Visakhapatnam.

'Contract and contractors document' shall mean the invitation of tenders, the stamped agreement, the specifications, the conditions and schedule of the contract.

'Month' means a month as reckoned by the English calendar.

'Site' shall mean and include all the areas in which any operation in respect of the work to be carried out. This includes the collection centres and the dumping ground.

The 'word' used as the singular shall include the plural or *vice versa* as per the context.

Part-2: Instructions to the Tenderer

1. No tender will be accepted without the deposit of the prescribed earnest money as per tender notification and its conditions in the form of Demand Draft.

2. Only sealed tenders are to be offered and no unsealed tenders will be accepted.

3. The tenderer shall take utmost care and caution while filling up the tender and rates against the items mentioned in the schedule. No verification in the tender rates in the name, type, graphical, clerical mistake or misunderstanding, etc. at any stage will be accepted once the tender is submitted within the prescribed time.

4. The tender must be accompanied with the updated Income Tax Clearance certificate. Non-enclosure of this certificate will entail in the rejection of the offer/tender.

5. The tenderer shall state whether any of their partners is concerned in any capacity with any other company, firm, co-operative who is also filling tenders for the same work. Failing which and for incorrect statements, the tender will be rejected and the tenderer deposit forfeited and the tender/the contract will be cancelled at any stage and during its currency.

6. The rates shall be quoted per day both in figures as well as in words.

7. All corrections made in the tender must be attested by the tenderer.

8. The schedule issued to be used for one area only, different schedules are to be used for different areas.

Part-3: General Rules and Directions to the Tenderer

1. Tenderers are requested to sign the form of tender and schedule of rates. Tenders which are not signed accordingly shall be rejected.

2. The tenderers shall fill in invariably Annexure—duly filling in the columns. Non-adherence to this will disqualify the tenders for consideration.

3. No tender will be accepted, unless the full amount of the EMD (Earnest Money Deposit) is paid in time as required.

4. All tenderers must disclose the names of their partners if any and the address in capital letters and also mention their addresses and telephone numbers. Any tenderer failing to do so will render himself liable for disqualification and the EMD shall be forfeited and if the fact is noticed after he enters into the contract, the same will be cancelled at any time during its currency.

5. If it is found that two or more persons who are connected with one another either financially or as principal and agent of master and servant, have tendered separately under different names for the same contract without disclosing the connection, such tenders will be rejected and the tender deposits forfeited. Any contract entered into under such condition will be liable to be cancelled at any time during its currency.

6. No addition or alternation will be allowed in the schedule or tender conditions/contract.

7. The tender deposit together with such other deposit as may be made will be retained and held by the Commissioner till the terms of the contractor are fulfilled and subject to the conditions mentioned in the contract.

8. In the event of the tender being accepted, the contract must be signed by the societies registered under societies registration act or the person having the registered power of attorney specifically authorising him to sign on his behalf shall affix the signature accordingly.

9. The contract shall be entered into within 3 days by the tenderer from the date of receipt of the information of acceptance

of tender and failure to do so will be deemed to have contravened the terms and conditions of the contract.

10. In the case of joint stock company, the contract must be sealed with the corporate seal of the company in the presence of and signed by atleast two directors thereof.

11. The Commissioner, Greater Visakhapatnam Municipal Corporation, shall have liberty to reject the lowest offer or the tender on any ground.

12. It shall be incumbent on the successful tenderer to pay the stamp duty on the contract.

13. Tenderers must distinctly understand:

(a) That they will strictly conform to the conditions of the contract as contained in each of its clauses and the plan and custom prevailing will not, on any account, be admitted as a ground for excuse on their part or for infringement of any of these conditions.

(b) The postponement of the payment of the full contract deposit for execution of the contract will not be permitted on the reason that the Municipal Corporation is having in its persons deposits, and no such transfers of deposits shall be permitted.

14. The rates quoted shall be final and no variation will be allowed on any ground.

15. The Commissioner reserves the right to select one or more items of the same tender split up at his discretion without references to any other items of the tender and the contractor will require to comply with such decision of the rate tender of such items.

16. The contractors are bound by the specifications and terms and conditions.

17. The tender deposit shall be forfeited, if the tenderer withdraws the tender before the decision by the competent authority or in the event of its acceptance finds fault to execute the contract as required and the rate tendered shall be valid for 60 days.

18. The corporation will deduct at source the prevailing rates of the income tax as per the provisions of the Income Tax Act on the gross amount of each bill submitted (Present recovery @ 2%).

19. Each tender must be subscribed with:

(a) Tender notification number.

(b) Due date of the tender.

(c) Name of the work.

(d) Name of the tenderer.

20. The Commissioner has the right to reject any or all the tenders without assigning any reason.

21. Earnest Money Deposit of the unsuccessful tenderer will be returned as soon as possible and after the tender has been decided without any interest.

22. The bills for the contractor after satisfactory execution of the work, will be paid. The payment shall be made once in every month and the bill shall accompany the satisfactory certificate signed by the CMH. The Commissioner shall have power to impose any cut in the bill for non-satisfactory execution of any of the items of work at his discretion. Based on the satisfactory certificate issued by the CMOH/AMOH shall prepare the bill and submit for payment.

23. Failure to execute the work on any particular day will entail a penalty on percentage of the contract amount towards each of such default.

24. If the work turned out by the contractor is not satisfactory and found inadequate, a minimum of one per cent of fine will be levied. If this condition continues, fine proportionate to the degree of unsatisfactory work will be levied as decided by the Commissioner. If the contractor continues to be defaulter more than three times during the existence of the contractor period, the contract is liable for cancellation and the EMD shall be forfeited and the contractor will be black listed.

25. Failing to execute the work as per the terms and conditions and specification of the contract, the Commissioner

is at liberty without further notice to rescind the contract and entrust the same or any portion of the work to another tenderer or otherwise at the costs and risk of the contractor and refer claims for the difference in the rates and for all other expenses whatsoever have been incurred in entrusting the contract work, for which the corporation is authorised to recover any money due to the contractor in any bill or deposit on any account.

26. Rates on the schedules should be entered in words and figures in ink only and all corrections should be attested with date by the tenderer. If there is any difference in the rates quoted either in words or in any figures, the lowest will be taken into account.

27. The contractor shall be liable for all the damages caused by him or his men while executing the contract including any damage caused to public. The Commissioner shall estimate the extent of damage and require the same to be paid by the contractor, failing which the same will be recovered from the contractor for any sum that has become due or already due from the corporation under this contract or otherwise. If the decision in this regard is taken by the officer subordinate to the Commissioner, an appeal shall lie to the Commissioner whose decision there shall be final. The contractor shall bear all the expenses for defending any legal proceeding that may be brought by any person for injury sustained by his wing due to neglect or lack of precaution, and shall pay the damage and costs that may be awarded on account of this consequence.

28. The contractor shall not assign any portion or whole or sublease the contract. If the contract is assigned or sublet or an attempt to do so is made, or the contractor has become insolvent, or any proceedings are commenced against the contractor for adjudication as insolvent, or if any pecuniary help is offered otherwise either directly or indirectly, or premises are given as such by contract or any of his servants or his agents to any officer of the corporation or if any person employed by the corporation is directly or indirectly interested in the contract, the Commissioner thereupon, by the notice in writing, rescind the contract and the security deposit of the contractor shall

thereupon stand forfeited at the direction of the Commissioner and the same consequence shall ensure as if the contract has been rescinded. In addition, the contractor shall not be entitled to recover or to be paid for any work actually performed under the contract.

29. The contractor shall be responsible for and shall pay any compensation to his own workmen payable under the workman's compensation Act for the injuries caused to the workmen during the course of employment. If such, compensation has to be paid by corporation as principle under the said Act, it shall be recoverable by the corporation from the security deposit and EMD or any other payments payable to the contractor.

30. The contractor shall provide with personnel, all necessary safety requirement and first aid apparatus for the benefit of persons employed on the site and shall maintain the same in good condition suitable for immediate use at any time and shall comply with the following regulations connected therewith. No workmen or employees of the contractor engaged in the contract services of VMC shall have any right or claim of seeking any employment in the corporation by the virtue of any service rendered under the contract.

(a) The workers shall be required to use the equipment provided by the contractor and the contractor shall take adequate steps to ensure proper use of the equipment by all those concerned.

(b) When the work is carried on in proximity to any place where there is a risk of drawing all necessary equipment shall be provided and kept ready for use and all necessary steps shall be taken for the prompt rescue of any person in danger.

31. Adequate provision shall be made for prompt first aid treatment of all injuries likely to be sustained during the course of employment.

32. Payment of contractor will be made by crossed cheque.

33. In case of registered societies, the latest audit report and the audit certificate issued by the societies or any other

authorised authorities for this purpose shall be furnished along with the tenders. Tenders received without them will be automatically rejected.

34. All the above conditions shall be accepted by the successful tender before execution of the work.

35. The contractor shall engage the number of persons and no. of vehicles as mentioned in the schedule daily on the site of work, failing which proportionate amount will deducted from his running bills.

Then at the time of execution of agreement the tenderer was further asked to fulfill the following terms and conditions:

1. The EMD will also be forfeited by termination of the contract in case the contractor fails to start the work in accordance with the work order or fails to carry out the work satisfactorily as per the tender conditions and the terms and conditions of the contract.
2. The rate for each has to be indicated on daily basis and the bills have to be prepared once in a month after completion of the month and subject to other conditions stipulated in the tender form and agreement. The contractor shall take works on Sundays and public holidays.
3. The income tax that would be in force will be deducted from monthly payment bills of the successful tenderers.
4. The work includes sweeping of the roads, sub-lanes, bye-lanes, footpaths, road margins and other public open places and cleansing the drains in the possession of the corporation daily and collection, transportation and disposal of the garbage everyday to Kapuluppada dumping yard or any other place that would be indicated by the CMOH/AMOH and cleaning and disinfecting of the areas in and around the dustbins, collection centres, garbage houses everyday by using necessary disinfectants/ chemicals indicated by AMOH (bleaching powder, lime, etc. This includes the day-to-day collected silt in road margins and from drains.

5. The boundaries of the areas included in the schedule is subject to little changes or deviations in case of necessary conditions. However, the norms will remain unaltered.
6. All successful tender should enter into agreement within 3 days from the date of receipt of the intimation of the acceptance of the tender, failing which the tenderer is subject to be disqualified unless proper reasons are given in writing which will be decided at the discretion of the Commissioner.
7. The contractor should follow the norms indicated in the notification, tender form agreement with regard to employment of workers for cleaning and loading works.
8. The right of accepting or rejecting any or all the tenders without assigning any reasons is reserved with Commissioner/Standing Committee, GVMC.
9. Every month the contractor shall enclose with the claims the xerox copies of the necessary records which will be signed by the responsible persons residing just opposite to dustbin's point everyday.
10. The registration certificate from Labour Department shall be enclosed to the tender by all the intending tenderer.
11. Failure to execute the work daily with prescribed labour and vehicles, the Commissioner shall have power to deduct the proportionate amount of labour and vehicles from the bill amount.
12. The approved tenderer shall commence the work of street sweeping, cleaning the drains as well as lifting of garbage simultaneously everyday from 9 p.m. and complete the main roads first and subsequently other lanes, by-lanes, sub-lanes, with a total working hours of 8 hours/day.
13. The materials procured by the contractor is of good quality and the bleaching powder, etc., should be of standard make and with ISI certificate.

14. The corporation is not liable for any accidents, injuries, etc., occurred during transportation time.
15. The roads included for the work are subject to change or deviation in case of necessity without any alternation in the norms.
16. The contractors shall be responsible to ensure that the workers engaged in garbage removal operations shall not resort to burning of the garbage and other solid wastes on the road margins, footpaths, and near collection points as burning of such material may cause fire hazards besides pollution of the environment. The contractor shall be responsible to ensure that no garbage and other solid wastes are dumped in open drains and other water bodies as such dumping may lead to choking of drains and water contamination.
17. The contractor shall arrange to provide the required personal safety equipments like hand gloves, gum boots and masks to all the workers and ensure that they wear them during the garbage removal operations, and he shall also arrange to supply identification badges to all the workers engaged by him.
18. The contractor shall maintain the attendance registers for the workers engaged by him, maintain a pinpoint programme for cleaning. All the registers, records shall be maintained daily and shall be made available to the Municipal Authorities for inspection during regular checking.
19. The contractor shall ensure that no child labour is engaged on the execution of work failing which he shall be liable for prosecution under Child Labour Act.
20. The contractor shall possess the valid, labour licence issued by the department of labour and authentic copy of the licence shall be furnished along with the tender.
21. The contractor shall be responsible to observe the Contract Labour Act and the Minimum Wages Act during the execution of work.

22. The contractor shall undertake to arrange payment of wages to the workers at their respective ward offices in the presence of the officers authorised by the Commissioner, VMC.

COLLECTION AND TRANSPORTATION OF SOLID WASTES BY BENGALURU MAHANAGAR PALIKA (KARNATAKA)

The BMP (Bengaluru Mahanagar Palika) has also privatised the collection and disposal of municipal solid wastes in the sense that the task is handed over through open bidding to private bidders.

Instructions to Bidders

BMP has adopted a single stage bidding process for selection of the service provider to carry out collection and transportation of municipal solid waste and street sweeping in select health wards of BMP. The project is envisaged to be effective for a period of three(3) years from the date of signing of an agreement with BMP ("the Agreement"). The scope of work and commercial conditions in the project are well defined as follow:

Scope of Work and Commercial Conditions

The service provider shall carry out all the activities, in the package awarded, set out as Task A and Task B activities. BMP reserves the right to make changes (addition/deletion) in the area included in the package(s) awarded to the service provider. In case the service provider is registered under the Contract Labour (Regulation and Abolition) Act, 1970, the service provider shall submit to BMP a copy of such registration. If the service provider is not registered under the said Act, the service provider shall before undertaking the project, obtain a licence from the office of the labour commissioner and submit a copy of the same to BMP.

Scope of Work

BMP issues a letter of commencement of work only upon receipt of either a copy of the aforesaid certificate of registration or licence, as the case may be, issued by the office of the labour commissioner. The service provider shall be responsible to undertake, commence work and execute all activities indicated herein after receipt of letter of commencement of work from BMP.

Task A Activities

The scope of work of the service provider includes the following:

- Door to door collection of MSW from the generators such as households, commercial establishments, institutions, etc.
- The service provider shall collect MSW from the generators on a daily basis and as per implementation plan.
- During the term of the agreement, BMP may notify certain areas where MSW segregation (biodegradable and non-biodegradable) would be practiced by the generators. The service provider shall be required to collect and transport the biodegradable and non-biodegradable fractions of MSW and not mixed with each other at any stage.
- In such areas, the service provider shall collect the biodegradable MSW on a daily basis, while the non-biodegradable MSW shall be collected thrice a week (Sunday, Tuesday and Friday) after completing door to door collection of biodegradable MSW and as per the implementation plan.
- The service provider shall use either containerised pushcarts or auto tippers for collection of MSW from the generators for transportation of the MSW collected from the above generators to designated location notified by BMP from time to time ("Designated Locations"). The currently identified designated locations are at a distance of approximately 25 kilometres from Vidhana Soudha.
- The service provider shall carry out sweeping and collection of MSW from the markets and their surroundings areas in their package and transport the MSW collected to designated locations on a daily basis.
- The service provider shall carry out transportation of MSW collected from all the above sources in fully covered tipper lorries only.

Task B Activities

The scope of work of the service provider shall include the following:

Sweeping of roads, streets, footpaths and pavements and open roadside drains/mouth of shoulder drains.

- The sweeping of all the roads, streets, footpaths, pavements and cleaning of open roadside drains/mouth of shoulder drains shall be done from one end to the other end on a daily basis. All the vegetation and weeds on the roads, footpaths, pavements and open roadside drains/mouth of shoulder drains shall be uprooted on a regular basis as per the implementation plan and disposed off along with street sweepings collected.
- The sweeping work shall be done on a daily basis and the sweepings collected shall be transported on the same day to designated locations. The kerbs and the medians shall also be cleaned everyday. Care shall be taken that the sweeping activity does not hinder traffic movement on the roads.
- The service provider shall ensure that the transportation of the MSW collected from the generators and street sweepings and silt are not mixed and are transported separately to the designated locations.
- The service provider shall clean public toilets and urinals in their packages on a daily basis. The service provider shall be responsible for deployment of staff at such public toilets and for provision of water, disinfectants, etc.
- The service provider shall sweep and collect MSW, dry leaves, etc. from community bins, burial grounds, civic amenities sites and other such places in their package as per the implementation plan.
- The service provider shall deploy dedicated manpower, with a dress code decided in consultation with BMP, for clearing litter, carrying out mopping activities in the areas and the earmarked locations.

- The service provider shall clean open places of BMP owned buildings and toilets and parking space of such buildings and shall deploy staff for these activities, as required.
- The service provider shall collect MSW dumped in the vacant sites in the packages and transport the same to the designated locations.
- The service provider shall remove all posters, buntings and unauthorised banners and transport the same to designated locations.
- The service provider shall transport carcasses of dead animals found within the packages to the designated locations.

Other Conditions

- The service provider shall collect SWM cess from the generators as per the instructions/notification issued by BMP in this regard. The service provider shall deposit such amounts collected with BMP, as indicated in the instruction/notification. The service provider shall furnish to BMP list of generators who do not pay the said SWM cess.
- In case, the designated locations are changed resulting in a longer distance to be travelled, BMP shall make an additional payment of Rs. 10 per kilometre for every extra kilometre travelled over 50 kilometres (considering the onward and return of 25 kilometres each) travelled in the trip, to the service provider.
- The service provider shall provide and utilise vehicles and equipment as set out further for carrying out the activities set as above.
- The service provider shall designate and appoint suitable officers/representatives to supervise the project.
- The service provider shall ensure that the MSW collected under Task A and Task B activities are not mixed at any stage of collection and transportation.

- The service provider shall promote MSW segregation at household level through awareness campaigns and other suitable means.
- The service provider shall ensure that there is no spillage of MSW during collection from the generators and transportation to the designated locations.
- The service provider shall ensure that the collected MSW is not burnt or disposed off in any manner whatsoever.
- The service provider shall report non-compliance of MSW management practices by generators to BMP.
- The service provider shall maintain daily records of the quantum of MSW collected, transported, time schedule of performance of the activities envisaged in the agreement and other such relevant information. The same shall be provided to BMP on request.
- The service provider shall maintain a complaint register for registering the grievances of the generators and other stakeholders.
- The service provider shall obtain compliance certificate from citizens/BMP officials for monitoring and supervision of their works.
- The service provider shall be responsible for the safety and security of its employees and the plant and machinery deployed for execution of the project.
- In case, the service provider dumps/deposits MSW collected in its package area on such roads or areas, which do not form a part of his package except as directed by BMP, it shall pay, as penalty an amount equal to its service fee for each such instance.

Monitoring Mechanism

- A monitoring committee comprising the health officer, medical officers of health and shuchi mitras would be set up for each package to supervise the performance of the service provider. The committee would make regular/ spot inspections and evaluate the performance of the service provider on following indicators:

Collection of MSW either on a daily basis or as per the implementation plan.

Daily transportation of the MSW collected.

Littering of MSW in the package.

- The service provider shall obtain compliance certificate from at least 2 (two) shuchi mitras, or in their absence from prominent citizens, for performance of MSW collection activity from the generators, sweeping of streets, collection of loose stones, etc. on a daily basis. The shuchi mitras or the prominent citizens shall be selected by BMP on a rotation basis.
- BMP would provide the contact numbers of the shuchi mitras in the monitoring committee to the generators in the package areas. The generators would file complaints against a service provider in the event of non-compliance in any of the activities envisaged under the agreement for more than one day continuously.
- BMP officials would carry out inspection of the entire city from time to time. BMP through commissioner/ special commissioner, would declare the package which is the cleanest in the preceding month as "Parishudda Pradesha". The service provider of the package shall be awarded a cash prize of Rs. 15,000 (Rupees fifteen thousand only) along with a certificate of merit for having maintained cleanliness of the package at required levels.
- The service provider must accompany BMP officials as and when called upon during the visits of the latter to the service provider.

Payment Terms

- BMP shall pay to the service provider a stipulate amount as service fee per month.
- The service provider shall be required to submit bills and compliance certificate by 7th(seventh) day of every month. BMP upon verification of the same shall, within 30 days, release payments to the service provider after

deducting taxes as payable under applicable law and after taking into account any deductions/fine/penalties imposed by BMP.

- In case of dispute, the undisputed amount will be paid and the disputed amount will be verified and if found in order shall be paid along with the bills for the following month.
- All payments to the service provider shall be made by way of account payee cheque drawn in favour of the service provider.

Time Schedules for Implementation of Works

The service provider shall adhere to the time schedule set out as below for implementation of the project:

Sl. No.	Activity	Time Schedule
1.	Door to door collection of MSW from various households	7:00 a.m. to 11:00 a.m.
2.	Street Sweeping:	
	Main roads identified in consultation with BMP	6:30 a.m. to 8:30 a.m.
	Other roads in the package	6:30 a.m. to 9:30 a.m.
3.	Collection of MSW from the markets, commercial establishments and transportation	8:00 a.m. to 12 noon and 3:00 p.m. to 7:00 p.m.
4.	Cleaning of urinals, BMP owned building and other such places	7:30 a.m. to 11:30 a.m.
5.	Transportation of MSW and street sweepings to designated locations	7:30 a.m. to 1:30 p.m.
6.	Deployment of staff at earmarked locations	9:00 a.m. to 9:00 p.m.

Tools, Equipment and Vehicles to be Provided by the Service Provider

The service provider shall provide the following tools, equipment and vehicles for implementation of the project:

- Auto tippers
- Pushcarts with bells and four containers
- Long handle brooms
- Metal tray with scrappers
- Baskets

- Drainage scrappers
- Gumboots
- Hand gloves
- Black phenyl
- Iron forks
- Mumtees
- Water tanker with jetpumps
- Tipper lorries

BMP invites proposals from interested parties for the project in order to identify the successful bidder for each package. The proposals would be valuated on the basis of the set out criteria.

- Each bidder shall submit a maximum of 1(one) proposal for each package. Any bidder, who submits more than one proposal for a package shall be disqualified. While the bidders may submit proposals for one or more of the packages, a maximum of two(2) packages shall be awarded to each successful bidder.
- The bidder shall pay for all the costs associated with the preparation of its proposal and its participation in the bidding process.

Eligible Bidders

- The bidders eligible for participation in the qualification process shall be individual/partnership firm/company incorporated under the Companies Act, 1956.
- The bidder shall furnish a declaration to BMP to the effect that it does not attract ineligibility of the provisions under section 26 of the KMC Act, 1976 or any of the provisions of Karnataka Civil Services (CCA) Rules, 1957.
- Each bidder shall submit a power of attorney authorising the signatory of the proposal to commit the bidder.

Earnest Money Deposit (EMD)

- The bidder shall submit EMD of Rs. 3,00,000 (Rupees three lakhs only) for each package in the form of a crossed demand draft/banker's cheque drawn on any scheduled bank, in favour of the Commissioner, Bengaluru Mahanagar Palika payable at Bengaluru.

- EMD of every unsuccessful bidder would be returned within a period of 30(thirty) days from the date of announcement of the successful bidder for each package. The EMD submitted by the successful bidder would be released upon furnishing of the performance security, amounting to 10 per cent of the contract value (service fee payable by BMP to the service provider during the agreement period) by way of an irrevocable bank guarantee, issued by a scheduled bank located in India in favour of commissioner, Bengaluru Mahanagar Palika, payable at Bengaluru, for due and punctual performance of the obligations relating to the project.

Format and Signing of Proposal

- The bidder would provide all the necessary informations as per this RFP. BMP would evaluate only those proposals that are received in the required format and are complete in all respects. Each proposal shall have a technical offer and a financial offer separately.

Privatisation of Sanitation in SAS Nagar/Mohali (Punjab)

The shortage of safai sevaks (sweepers) in the towns had been increasing over the years. Due to resource crunch, usually no new recruitment has been done after the retirement of regular staff. Sanitation work, therefore, suffered and privatisation was proposed as a solution to the problem.

SAS Nagar (Mohali, Punjab) Municipal Council introduced privatisation of sanitation in certain parts of the city in the year 2000 for eight months on an experimental basis and the results were found to be satisfactory. The people were generally satisfied with sanitation conditions. The areas were cleaner and the private contractor's men were available on call. In May 2001, it is reported that 20 parties responded to the tender notice of the Council for the one year sanitation contract but only 10 were found eligible. The ten contractors were assigned the different areas for cleaning of roads, streets, parks, open spaces and for daily lifting of garbage. The parties concerned had quoted rates slightly lower than the estimated cost fixed by the council.

The Executive Officer said that the contractor's men would have to carry an identity card with them. If any worker was found working without his identity card, a fine of Rs. 100 would be imposed. If the sanitation work of any contractor were not found satisfactory, the council would impose a penalty amounting to 10 per cent of the contract money. In Nangal town (District Ropar, Punjab) also, the sanitation work has been divided between the council and the private parties. The system had proved to be satisfactory there also. Some of the contractors would be using their own machinery while the others want to use the machinery of the council. However, at the time of making payment the council would go in for the necessary deductions for the use of its machinery.

The council has worked out the number of employees that each contractor would have to engage in the zone. The municipal authorities have appealed to the residents of the town to make a written complaint if the employees of the contractor do not sweep the streets in their area daily so that action can be taken against the concerned contractor. But if no proper checking is done by the municipal authority and the people of the concerned area, then the contractor's men do not work upto the desired mark.

Some residents allege that the council had washed its hands of the responsibility of collecting and disposing the garbage by asking the residents to make arrangements for throwing the garbage at earmarked sites making their own private arrangement. Therefore, there appears to be a dire need for strengthening the system of door to door garbage collection. And the residents can be asked to make a paltry contribution of Rs. 10-20 per month. This charge can also be included in water bill wherever feasible.

S.A.S. Municipal Council scrapped the sanitation contract on January 6, 2004 as the contractor failed to improve the sanitation conditions even after repeated warnings. Municipal Council, therefore, deducted Rs. 57.4 thousand, Rs. 1.96 lakhs, Rs. 1.56 lakhs, Rs. 1.09 lakhs and Rs. 2.08 lakhs from July,

August, September, October and November installments. The contractor had not been engaging the number of employees as specified in terms of agreement and was also not regularly lifting garbage from certain areas. Sanitary contractors generally used to employ far less workers as stipulated in contract while charging municipal bodies for the entire staff. Other things like issuing I-cards and dress to the workers were never implemented. Sometimes even the municipal bodies also did not fulfill their promise of providing tractor trolley for the refuse to collectors and payment in time. Therefore, some checks also need to be imposed for municipal body.

The successful privatisation of most works of civic body has also encouraged other local bodies department to emulate this experiment in other parts of the State. For example, though privatisation of all works, except fire services, of the newly constituted Panchkula Municipal Committee (Haryana) was done to meet the paucity of funds, it is now being seen as a model to be implemented in the civic bodies of other cities. Privatisation has not only reduced the financial burden of the municipal committees, but the private contractors are also more accountable for better services for fear of their contract being cancelled.

Chandigarh Municipal Corporation (U.T.) has launched garbage-free sectors scheme. Residents of the city have urged the M.C. to evolve certain inherent mechanism to ensure the success of garbage-free sectors scheme. They have suggested that charges for the collection of garbage from door to door be included in the water bill to ensure that the beneficiaries pay for the services.

The system of collecting garbage from doorsteps and dumping it at the "Sehaj Safai Kendras" has not been functioning smoothly. People, who have refused to pay the safai karamchari, prefer to dump the garbage at roadsides. Some residents have alleged that the corporation has merely washed its hands of the responsibility of collecting and disposing of the garbage by asking the resident welfare associations to make arrangements for throwing the garbage at earmarked sites even though the kendras are yet to come up. Mayor of the municipal corporation said that corporation did not have the manpower to take over the job of garbage collection from house to house. The gigantic task of collecting garbage from the houses, collection of garbage charges, payment of wages to the safai karamchari, repair and upkeep of rehris and keeping an account of the money was very time consuming.

The residents have urged that the corporation must ensure that the Sehaj Safai Kendras may be constructed before implementing the garbage-free sectors scheme. The 'Kendras' should not be constructed on the basis of a standard design but its size and design should depend upon the number of houses from where the garbage and other household refuse was to be collected. In case the residents fail to pay for garbage collection charges, the corporation should include the charges in the water bill as sanitation cess. To ensure the sweeping of roads, a list of the sweepers should be available with the councillors and the executive bodies of the resident welfare associations.

Municipal Corporation, Chandigarh, under the pressure from the sweeper's union and due to some other reasons decided that contract system in sanitation wing, should not be pursued further. The nine member special committee of the Chandigarh M.C. in its report rejected the proposal of initiating contract system for sanitation work in the city. Further, suggesting the scrapping of the scheme under the prevailing conditions, the corporation has recommended to the General House that "the contract system in the sanitation wing of the M.C. does not appear to be properly workable to ensure good sanitation conditions. Hence, the private contract system in the sanitation wing may not be pursued for the time being." The report has also suggested to engage sweepers on daily wages (on contract) as per the requirement of the corporation by providing them minimum wages to ensure proper sanitation of the city. If the corporation, to ensure proper sanitation of the city, finds that proper sanitary conditions are not being maintained, it may adopt any other suitable alternative method to ensure proper sanitation. Political observers say that the corporation has mainly stressed the need to pacify the sweepers, who had been showing their uneasiness over the issue, following apprehensions of losing their jobs.

The system of door to door garbage collection was introduced in some cities a few years ago by voluntary organisations in an attempt to solve the waste disposal problem. The collectors, in lieu of reasonable amount, were in the business of gathering the waste from house to house before disposing of the same at an appropriate place.

In sectors where the private service was unavailable, the residents were throwing the garbage in 'haudies' constructed in front of the residences or even in the back lane or open space till the waste was collected by the corporation staff.

But with the introduction of bin-free sectors and the refusal of the corporation authorities to collect the garbage from the 'haudies' the concept of door to door collection of garbage assumed greater significance. Aware of the problem, the corporation officials assert that the problem will continue till the residents welfare associations are taken into confidence. Public participation is must if such projects are to be made a success.

In Chandigarh, the private garbage collectors, gathering waste from house to house, have hiked their charges (from Rs. 25 to Rs. 50) in most of the bin-free sectors leading to resentment among the residents. The extra money is being charged on the pretext of carrying 'horticulture waste' that the residents allege.

Some residents add that the collectors are openly blackmailing them by asserting that "pay or we will stop collecting the garbage". The collectors openly threaten the residents. As the areas have been divided between the different collectors and entry of outsiders into the business is strictly prohibited, the residents are hardly left with any option but to pay more. The corporation need to evolve certain strategies to ensure against blackmailing by collectors.

Privatisation of municipal services was done to reduce the financial burden of the councils and to improve the services, as the private contractors are more accountable. Further, whenever any aberration in the work of a contractor is found, the M.C.

can impose fines on them. But even this deterrent has not reportedly helped in improving things. Therefore, the municipal authorities have to explore other alternatives for carrying out the works, keeping in mind the constraints of staff and finances. Active involvement of the resident beneficiaries should also be ensured while operating such services are essential for maintaining proper sanitation.

Mohalla (Street) Sanitation Scheme in Urban Local Bodies

Mohalla Sanitation Scheme has been introduced in some areas of municipal corporations/councils/nagar panchayats, where proper sanitation arrangements are lacking. This scheme has been introduced in order to meet the increasing demand of sanitation in the towns. The public response to this scheme where it has been introduced has been encouraging. The salient features of this scheme are:

(a) No person would be required to clean daily more than one thousand meters of length of 'pacca' roads, 'pacca' streets or 'pacca' bazaar, or eight hundred metres length of 'kacha' road, 'kacha' street or 'kacha' bazaar. If appointed on cleaning drainage, his beat shall not exceed one thousand metres length of drain or intercepting drain. If employed for removal of rubbish, the load to be carried in one trip shall ordinarily be fifteen kilograms and the total beat shall not exceed two and a half kilometres. In case the rubbish is carried through wheel barrowers, the load shall be as per the capacity of the wheel barrow.

(b) The beat fixed in above shall be subject to the condition that the width of the road, street or bazaar to be cleaned does not exceed six metres. If the width of the road, street or bazaar exceeds or is less than six metres, the length of the beat shall be enhanced or reduced proportionately.

(c) A committee of atleast three persons duly elected by the inhabitants of the concerned mohalla shall be constituted under the supervision of a representative of the Municipal Council.

Scope of the Scheme

(i) The scope of the scheme will cover all extended or leftover areas of the urban local bodies where there is inadequacy in the sanitation services. The area of operation will confine to the limits of urban local body concerned. The municipal corporations/councils/nagar panchayats will participate in the scheme only to the extent of providing financial assistance to the Mohalla Sanitation Committee. The sweepers engaged for this purpose by those committees will be exclusively on their rolls and they shall not be deemed to be the employees of urban local bodies.

(ii) Concerned Municipal Councillor, Executive Officer or the representative shall have the right to inspect the sanitation work.

Constitution of the Committee

The Mohalla Sanitation Committee will consist of at least three members, President, Secretary, Cashier. This committee will be constituted unanimously by the inhabitants of the mohalla. In case of disagreement the election of the said committee will he held under the supervision of concerned Sanitary Inspector, and any dispute in the conduct of election shall be referred to the concerned Executive Officer in the case of urban local bodies and officer incharge of sanitation branch in case of corporation whose decision shall be final. No appeal shall lie to any higher authority against his decision.

Engagement of Safai Karamchari

The Safai Karamcharis will be engaged by the Mohalla Sanitation Committee and he/they will be absolutely under the control of Mohalla Sanitation Committee only.

Approval and Adoption by the Local Bodies

The scheme on adoption by the concerned local body shall be deemed to have been administratively approved. The adoption of scheme shall be through a resolution of the concerned municipality.

Sweeping Equipments

The sweeping equipments like wheel barrow(s), brooms, panjer, tasla, tokra, etc. shall be provided to the sweeper by the concerned Mohalla Sanitation Committee. A lump sum grant of Rs. 2500 per year shall be provided by the concerned ULBs for the purpose.

Finance

(i) The Mohalla Sanitation Committee will be the overall incharge of all financial matters such as the payment of wages and collection of voluntary funds from the residents of the beat area. The Executive Officer on behalf of the municipality will provide Rs. 1200 per month as share money as grants-in-aid to the concerned Mohalla Sanitation Committee, if the sanitation area is equal to that of beat (+5%). An equal amount of Rs. 1200 per month may be provided by the Mohalla Committee concerned. The grants-in-aid for the next month shall only be released by the concerned local body after the submission of utilisation certificate to the Executive Officer of the ULBs, duly signed by the President/ Secretary of the said committee in respect of the grants-in-aid of the previous month.

(ii) The ULBs will be at liberty to stop the grant at any time thereafter if this arrangement does not work satisfactorily.

(iii) The grant will be released on the recommendations of the Sanitary Inspector or representative of the Urban Local Bodies who will record a certificate as per performa or the certificates attached with the scheme.

Operation of Bank Accounts

Each Mohalla Sanitation Committee shall open a bank account in any nationalised/scheduled bank suitable to them. The account will jointly be operated by the President and any one member of the committee. The sanitary inspector or representative of urban local bodies of the area shall forward specimen signature of the office bearers of the committee to the concerned local body as well as to the bank concerned. The grants-in-aid will be disbursed by the concerned local body to the Mohalla Sanitation Committee by means of an account payee cheque. The accounts shall be kept by the concerned Mohalla Sanitation Committee in accordance with the procedure evolved by themselves and shall be open to inspection by the representative of the Urban Local Bodies or any member of the Beat Area.

REFERENCES

1. Rao, S. Bhoopathi and Abdul Sameen Ansari (2005).
2. *Ibid.*
3. *Ibid.*

Privatisation of Street Lighting and Other Services

4

Apart from the privatisation of octroi and urban waste management, the ULBs have also started contracting out many other public utility services like street lighting, construction and maintenance of public toilets, upkeep of city parks, water supply, city transport, education, medical services, etc. In this chapter, an attempt has been made to examine the operationalisation of some of these services.

Privatisation of Street Lighting

In Patiala city, the Municipal Corporation gave the work for the maintenance of streetlights on contract basis from November, 2002. After the privatisation, the functioning of streetlight did improve. On the other hand, the expenditure by the Municipal Corporation on streetlight has reduced. Prior to privatisation, Municipal Corporation had to incur Rs. 13 per point on maintenance cost, but after the privatisation maintenance cost was reduced to Rs. 6.50 per point. Prior to privatisation, 60-70 per cent of the streetlight points were functional, but after the privatisation 90-95 per cent of the points became functional as the contractor could be held responsible for the non-functioning of the streetlight points. As per the agreement clause, the contractor would ensure that no streetlight point remains out of order for more than 24 hours from the receipts/registration of complaint in the corporation/contractor's office. If the contractor defaults to maintain the streetlight properly or is unable to replace the defective points within 24 hours, he can be penalised as per agreed clause. But prior to privatisation, no one could be held responsible for the non-functioning of the streetlight points and on the other hand there was no proper patrolling for monitoring the working of the streetlight. However, some people do complain that there was not much improvement in the functioning of streetlight in their areas even after privatisation. The contractor also tends to concentrate mostly in VIP areas. They do not bother to repair the defective points in other localities. Generally, people are of the view that privatisation is better if proper checking and monitoring of the work done by the contractor is held regularly.

Terms and Conditions

1. The contractor is required to ensure that the street light system in the city is operated/maintained properly.
2. The contractor would be responsible for due upkeep of the streetlight points including lamps, tubes and other structures/feeding lines/damaged cables, etc.
3. The contractor will employ adequate numbers of streetlight patrollers for monitoring the working of the streetlight points and registering complaints thereof at a central place of each PSEB sub-division with proper records. For the purpose, contractor would also liaise with concerned corporation staff and officers for daily compilation of complaints.
4. The contractor will provide sufficient number of skilled labourers, ladders, kits and required safety measure instruments at his own level.
5. The contractor will provide the list of employees who must be technically qualified and will supervise the streetlight point and he will submit the daily report of non-functional streetlight points to the concerned in-charge.
6. The contractor must have a licence from the Chief Electrical Inspector, Punjab.
7. The contractor would ensure that no streetlight point remains out of order for more than 24 hours from the receipt/registration of complaint in the corporation/ contractor's office.

8. The contractor shall provide tubes/fittings/cables, etc. only of such standard or makes as Phillips, Crompton, Bajaj and cables (ISI marked) of standard manufactures like ICL, Gloster, Universal, etc.
9. If the contractor defaults to maintain the streetlight points properly or is unable to replace the defective points/feeding lines within 24 hours, he will be penalised @ Rs. 50 per point per day. This penalty amount shall be deducted from his running payments.
10. If at the time of taking over the work by the contractor any points are found inoperative, corporation will make them operative and will be jointly inspected by staff of corporation and contractor.
11. The contractor shall on the completion/termination of the contract hand over the complete streetlight system including fittings/structures/wires, etc. as existing at the time of start of work and also in respect of such points/ lines which get added during the contract period in absolute working conditions.
12. The contractor shall not have any authority to change the site/nature of the streetlight points without the prior permission of the Corporation Engineer/Officer duly authorised.
13. Running payments shall be made in the first fortnight of next month.
14. Security amount @ 10 per cent of the billed amount every month shall be deducted and the same shall be paid on the completion/termination of the contract after recovery of dues, if any.
15. In the event of any streetlight point getting abandoned for any reason or is required to be disconnected/ dismantled/ shifted, the material erected in respect of such point(s) shall be returned to the Corporation. However, neither any penalty shall be leviable on the party on account of the said inoperative point(s) nor any amount shall be payable to the contractor for such points till new point is installed thereof. The amount to be calculated for the

purpose shall be as per the point rates to be quoted by the contractor.

16. In case the contractor fails to restore particular streetlight points within a week period, corporation shall be at liberty to carryout restoration of the concerned point(s) at its own level and deduct the cost of the such work (including labour/supervision/administrative charges) from the contractor's bills besides the penalty amount as per the agreed clause.
17. In the event of any new points required to be created, it shall be done with the prior permission of the Commissioner, Municipal Corporation, Patiala and cost of such works shall be payable to the contractor as per the item rate to be quoted separately or as per CSR whichever is lower. However, the operation/maintenance charges shall be payable only for the remaining period during the calendar year on pro-rata basis.
18. The contract shall be operative only for one year initially from the date of award of the contract but can be extended with mutual consent.
19. The electricity consumption charges shall be payable to the PSEB by the corporation.
20. The contractor will be responsible for switching "off" and "on" of the streetlight system and maintain scheduled timing fixed by the municipal corporation. In case the contractor fails to switch off the streetlight system, he will be liable to pay the difference of energy wasted, calculated on the basis of connected load for the period of default. Inventory of the materials, mentioning make of the equipment, will be prepared and will be signed by the corporation as well as the contractor.
21. Numbering of the streetlight points will be done by the contractor as per corporation coding system within 15 days of taking over the contract.
22. The layout of the streetlight points shall be prepared by the contractor indicating the source of supply and the points fed from a particular streetlight feeds.

23. If at any stage new point(s) is required to be created, the contractor shall have to provide the same, the charges for such a new work shall be payable as per CSR or quoted item rate, whichever is lower.
24. The contract can be terminated by giving 15 days notice in case the performance of the firm/contractor is not found satisfactory and the earnest money shall be forfeited besides recovery of penalty charges leviable as per the agreed clauses.
25. The contractor shall be responsible for any accident/ mishappening resulting during operation/maintenance of the streetlight system to any of his staff or member of the public on account of any defective material supplied by him or bad workmanship or negligence on his part.
26. The contractor will not remove any installed materials from the site of work without prior approval of the competent authority.
27. In case the material is damaged/lost by accident/theft, the contractor shall intimate in writing to XEN/SDO/JE immediately and install the lost new material at site within five days failing which penalty @ Rs. 1000 per day per point will be charged.
28. Insurance of electricians, skilled labour, etc. is to be arranged by the contractor at his own level. In case of any accident, contractor will immediately intimate to XEN/ SDO/JE of municipal corporation as well as Chief Electrical Inspector, Punjab. Compensations, if any, will be paid by the contractor himself to the worker or his kin.
29. In the event of any dispute and/or disagreement and interpretation of any of the clauses of the agreement between parties, the Commissioner, Municipal Corporation, Patiala shall be the arbitrator and his decision shall be final and binding on both parties.
30. The contractor will arrange permits, etc., for working on lines from PSEB at his own level.

31. Contractor shall provide three sub-offices in the area with three sub-telephone facilities where public may contact and lodge the complaints.
32. The contractor strictly as per Indian Electricity Act/Rules will do all the works.
33. The special terms and conditions shall supersede, if laid down later on/during the period of contract, where the former comes into conflict with the latter.
34. All instructions/guidelines issued from time to time by the corporation relating to proper upkeep of streetlight system shall be binding on the contractor.
35. All legal proceedings in connection with the contract shall be subject to the territorial jurisdiction of the Civil Courts at Patiala only.
36. The other terms and conditions which are not covered under above conditions but are mentioned in the tender document will be applicable and binding on the contractor.
37. That the MW-4 form prepared under rule XIII (2) of the Municipal Account Code, 1930 shall form the part of this contract agreement, under which the contractor has to complete the work.
38. If the PSEB will add/alter any clause in the agreement, it will be binding on the contractors.
39. The increase in points, if any shall be permitted only after the approval of the F&CC and a separate agreement shall be executed for the same.

Privatisation of Drinking Water

Drinking water is the most basic element for human existence. The frequent droughts are further compounding the problem in many parts of the country. Even in states like Punjab and Haryana where adequate ground water is available, the rapidly declining water level is making its availability unsustainable. Then, there is the problem of availability of safe drinking water. Unfortunately, very scant efforts are being made to conserve this precious source of human existence. Its free distribution and even unmetred supply (i.e., charging at flat rates) by the state-owned and municipal agencies has led to great waste in its use. Many countries like France, however, have found ways to improve the efficiency by involving private sector participation in the supply of water for the poor, who are more concerned with water flowing from their taps than for small private profits.

In India, however, there is no evidence of privatising this precious commodity. But in many municipalities contracting out the dugging and operation of municipal tube wells, is practised whenever the demand for water shoots up. For example, in Pathankot (Punjab), it was observed that during the summer season, workers were employed on contract basis for 2-3 months to operate the additional municipal tube wells so that the supply of drinking water is kept uninterrupted.

Maintenance of City Parks

Many municipal corporations/bodies have also started privatising the upkeep and maintenance of city parks. Private parties, through open bidding, are asked to maintain the proper upkeep of parks and in return they are free to display their advertisements, or earn from selling the advertisements of other products at the designated places of the park. They can also earn from levying parking fees on private vehicles visiting the parks. Out of these earnings, they are supposed to deposit a fixed proportion with the municipal corporation/bodies.

Government can also outsource/privatise toiletry services and wherever it is not possible for the municipal bodies to do so, they can earmark certain places in the main market for public conveniences. Let the municipalities construct these toilets and their upkeep and maintenance can be entrusted to private parties in lieu of the advertisement rights given to them on contract basis. To ensure proper implementation of the contracts, some securities/bonds must be secured from the contractors and fines imposed in case of any lapse.

Privatisation of Other Services

Similarly, in Gurgaon (Haryana) many services like toilets, guide maps, foot over-bridge, display boards on poles, kiosk, unipoles, traffic booths and traffic posts, dustbins, bus shelters, tree guards, etc. have been outsourced. Under the new dispensation, expenditure would be borne by private advertisement agencies to provide world class facility to the public. The municipal corporation, Gurgaon would not have to bear any cost rather it will earn over Rs. 80 crores per annum by outsourcing these services.

Recently, even the Patiala Corporation (Punjab) has decided to privatise the upkeep and maintenance of traffic lights in the city in lieu of the advertisement rights given to the private parties.

5

Urban Development Schemes

Cities are the forerunners in economic development but due to heavy influx of rural population to urban areas, there is a great strain on the already scanty urban amenities. As per 2001 census, 28.50 crore population i.e., 27.8 per cent of the total reside in cities and this is likely to increase to 40 per cent in terms of GNP. Cities are likely to contribute 65 per cent by 2011. Thus whereas the contribution of urban population to economic development is increasing, their living conditions are not improving to that extent. Thus all-out efforts have to be made by all the concerned institutions, notably by the central, state and local-self governments to stem the rot in this regard. The Government of India has taken the initiative by introducing the following schemes:

(A) Jawaharlal Nehru National Urban Renewable Mission (JNNURM)

(B) Urban Infrastructure Development Schemes for Small and Medium Towns (UIDSSMT)

(C) Integrated Housing and Slums Development Programme (IHSDP)

(A) Jawaharlal Nehru National Urban Renewable Mission (JNNURM)

The scheme was introduced in 2005-06 and will remain operation for seven years. The Government of India has set apart Rs. 1,00,000 crore for the purpose. Under the scheme, the Central, State and Local grants will be given to the ULBs and parastatal agencies. The main objective of the JNNURM is to promote rapid reforms and integrated urban development by involving citizens, NGOs, ULBs, etc. in capacity building and providing urban amenities. For different categories of cities the provision of grants are as follows:

Type of city	Grants (Share of)		Local self-government
	Centre	State	
Cities with more than 40 lakh population (As per 2001 Census)	35%	15%	50%
Cities with more than 10 lakh but less than 40 lakh population (As per 2001 Census)	50%	20%	30%
U.T., State Capitals, Religious, Historical, Tourists and Other Cities	80%	10%	10%
Cities of North-Eastern and J&K States	90%	10%	—

Eligible Cities for Assistance Under JNNURM

1. According to 2001 census, the number of cities with more than 4 million population = 7.
2. According to 2001 census, the number of cities with more than 1 million but less than 4 million population = 28.
3. U.T., State capitals, Religious, Historical, Tourist and Other cities = 28.

Eligible Schemes for Urban Infrastructure

1. Urban renewables aimed at reconstruction of old areas and widening of narrow lanes; shifting of industrial and commercial enterprises from congested non-conforming areas inside the city to conforming areas outside the city; changing the old and worn out smaller pipes by new large capacity pipes; disposal of solid waste management, etc.
2. Water supply (including distillation) and cleanliness.
3. Sewerage and Solid Waste Management.
4. To construct and repair flood water and storm drains.
5. Urban transport including roads, highways, express ways, MRTC and metro projects.
6. Parking lots/spaces under PPP (Public Private Partnership).
7. Preservation of heritage buildings.

8. To protect the land from soil erosions in the states where the problem is common.
9. To conserve the water bodies.

Eligible Schemes for providing Basic Amenities to the Urban Poor

1. Rehabilitation and development of collective infrastructure in urban slums.
2. Schemes to provide basic amenities to the urban poor.
3. Rehabilitation of schemes for slum improvements.
4. Schemes relating to water supply sewerage, drainage, community toilets and bathrooms, etc.
5. Schemes of low cost housing for the slum dwellers, urban economically water sections (EWS) and low income groups (LIG).
6. Construction and repair of flood water and other drains.
7. Environmental improvements in the disposal of solid wastes management.
8. Street lighting.
9. Collective facilities like child care centres.
10. Administration and maintenance of assets created under this scheme.
11. A mixture of social security schemes relating to health education for the urban poor.

Ineligible Schemes under JNNURM

1. Electricity
2. Telecom
3. Health
4. Education and employees organisation
5. Employment Schemes
6. To create new employment opportunities.

(B) Urban Infrastructure Development Scheme for Small and Medium Towns (UIDSSMT)

Introduction

Urban Infrastructure Development Scheme for Small and Medium Towns aims at improvement in urban infrastructure in towns and cities in a planned manner. It shall subsume the existing schemes of Integrated Development of Small and Medium Towns (IDSMT) and Accelerated Urban Water Supply Programme (AUWSP).

Objectives

The objectives of the scheme are to:

(i) Improve infrastructural facilities and help create durable public assets and quality oriented services in cities and towns.

(ii) Enhance public-private partnership in infrastructural development.

(iii) Promote planned integrated development of towns and cities.

Duration of the Scheme

Like the JNNURM, the duration of this scheme will also be for seven years beginning from 2005-06. An evaluation of the outcomes of the scheme will be undertaken before the commencement of the 11th Five Year Plan and if necessary, the scheme would be suitably calibrated.

Coverage

The scheme will apply to all cities/towns as per 2001 census, excepting cities/towns covered under Jawaharlal Nehru National Urban Renewal Mission (JNNURM).

Allocation of funds among states will be on the basis of the state's urban population (excluding cities covered under JNNURM) to total urban population in the country (excluding cities covered under JNNURM).

States may allocate funds to towns/cities based on similar formula. However, funds would be provided to only those towns and cities where elections to local bodies have been held and elected bodies are in position.

The state governments may prioritise towns and cities on the basis of their felt-need. While selecting towns, states would take into account existing infrastructure, population of scheduled castes/scheduled tribes and special problems like hilly terrain.

Components

The components for assistance under the scheme will include all urban infrastructure development projects including water supply and sewerage. Land cost will not be financed except for acquisition of private land for schemes/projects in the North Eastern States and hilly states viz. Himachal Pradesh, Uttaranchal and Jammu and Kashmir.

Admissible Components

The scheme will cover the following areas:

(i) Urban Renewal i.e. re-development of inner (old) city areas. This would include items like widening of narrow streets, shifting of industrial/commercial establishments from non-conforming (inner-city) to conforming (outer-city) areas to reduce congestion, replacement of old and worn-out water pipes by new/higher capacity ones, renewal of sewerage/drainage/solid waste disposal systems, etc.

(ii) Water supply (including distillation plants) and sanitation.

(iii) Sewerage and Solid Waste Management.

(iv) Construction and improvement of drains/storm water drains.

(v) Construction/Upgradation of roads, highways/expressways.

(vi) Parking lots/spaces on public-private partnership basis.

(vii) Development of heritage areas.

(viii) Prevention and rehabilitation of soil erosion/landslides only in case of special category states where such problems are common.

(ix) Preservation of water bodies.

Inadmissible Items

(i) Power and telecommunication works.

(ii) Rolling stock like buses and trams.

(iii) Health and educational institutions.

(iv) Urban transport.

(v) Wage employment programme and staff component.

(vi) Maintenance works.

While sanctioning projects for slum improvement, state level sanctioning committee would ensure that there has not been any duplication of efforts from other sources. For this purpose, the implementing agencies are required to submit requisite certificate.

Financing Pattern

The sharing of funds would be in the ratio of 80:10 between central government and state government and the balance 10 per cent could be raised by the nodal/implementing agencies from the financial institutions. Implementing agencies may substitute internal resources for funds to be raised from financial institutions. However, in case of cities/towns in North Eastern states and Jammu and Kashmir, sharing of funds would be in the ratio of 90:10 between central and state government.

The state level sanctioning committee may sanction projects upto three times of central share subject to availability of funds. The committee would assign higher priority to projects of (i) Water supply (including distillation plants) and sanitation, (ii) Sewerage and Solid Waste Management, (iii) Road Network and (iv) Construction and improvement of drains/storm water drains.

Cities/towns/parastatals will be sanctioned project-based grants/loans which in turn would leverage, to the extent, the loan component/state share could be suitably reduced.

The scheme will be implemented through a designated state level nodal agency.

Release of Central Assistance

Central assistance (grant) released will go directly to the nodal agencies identified by the state government as additional central assistance.

Release of central share to nodal agency will be in two installments and will depend on availability of state share and submission of utilisation certificates within 12 months of the closure of the financial year in accordance with the provisions of General Financial Rules.

The criteria for release of funds will be as under:

- Fifty per cent of the central share will be released on signing of memorandum of agreement to the state nodal agency, after ascertaining availability of states share.
- Balance 50 per cent of the central share would be released on submission of utilisation certificates by nodal agency for 70 per cent of funds (central and state grants) released earlier.
- State level nodal agency will, however, release funds in the following manner:
  - Twenty-five per cent of central grant on ascertaining availability of state share.
  - Balance central grant after release of state grant and after assessment of progress of implementation of reforms.

Revolving Fund

The grant from Government of India and state government will flow to the nodal agency designated by state government. The nodal agency will disburse central assistance to ULBs or parastatal agencies as the case may be, as soft loan or grant-cum-loan. However, in case of sanction of loan or grant-cum-loan, the same may be sanctioned in such a manner that 25 per cent of central and state grant put together is recovered and ploughed into revolving fund to leverage market funds for financing further investment in infrastructure projects. At the end of the scheme period, the revolving fund may be graduated to a state urban infrastructure fund.

State level sanctioning committee would decide period of plough back of grant into the revolving fund.

State level sanctioning committee would sanction projects for infrastructural development of cities and towns out of revolving fund in the same manner as projects are sanctioned out of corpus created out of central and state grants.

Incentives

After due assessment of status of implementation of activities for which incentives are sought. State level sanctioning committee may sanction additional central grant upto a maximum of 5 per cent to incentives implementing agencies as indicated below:

- 1.5 per cent for preparation of detailed project report.
- 1.5 per cent for training and capacity building relating to project.
- 1 per cent for bringing about efficiencies in the projects.
- 1 per cent for adoption of innovative approaches and adoption of proven and appropriate technologies.

State Level Nodal Agency

The state government may designate any existing institution as nodal agency for implementation of the scheme.

The nodal agency will be responsible for the following:

(i) Inviting project proposals from ULBs/parastatal implementing agencies.

(ii) Techno-economic appraisal of the projects either through in-house expertise or by outside agencies through outsourcing.

(iii) Management of funds received from central and state governments.

(iv) Disbursement of the funds as per the financing pattern given in the guidelines.

(v) Furnishing of utilisation certificates with in 12 months of the closure of the financial year and quarterly physical and financial progress reports to the Ministry of Urban Development.

(vi) Maintenance of audited accounts of funds released to ULBs and implementing agencies.

(vii) Monitoring of implementation of reforms and infrastructure projects.

Project Appraisal

Urban Local Bodies and implementing agencies including parastatal agencies, will submit detailed project reports to the designated state level nodal agencies for appraisal.

The state level nodal agency will forward the appraised projects to MOUD, Planning Commission and TCPO so as to reach at least 15 days before the meeting of state level sanctioning committee for enabling their representatives to offer their comments/views on the projects in the meeting.

State Level Sanctioning Committee (SLSC)

The Composition of the State Level Sanctioning Committee (SLSC) may be as follows:

Secretary, Urban Development/Municipal Admn./Local Self-Governments:	Chairman
Secretary, Finance	Member
Secretary, Planning	Member
Secretary, Works/Engineer-in-Chief of PWD	Member
Director (Town and Country Planning)/ Chief Town Planner of the State	Member
Representative of M/o Urban Development	Member
Representative of I.F. Division, M/o Urban Dev.	Member
Representative of Planning Commission	Member
Representative of TCPO	Member
Representative of NCR Planning Board, New Delhi (in case of states of Haryana, Uttar Pradesh and Rajasthan)	Member
Chief Executive of the State Level Nodal Agency	Member-Secretary

SLSC will ensure the following:

(a) Examine and approve project reports submitted by the local bodies/implementing agencies including parastatal agencies, taking into account the appraisal reports. The committee will assign higher priority to projects relating to water supply including sanitation, sewerage, solid waste management, road network and drainage.

(b) Periodically monitor the progress of sanctioned projects/schemes including funds mobilisation from financial institutions.

(c) Review the implementation of the scheme keeping in view its broad objectives and ensure that the programmes taken up are in accordance with guidelines laid down.

(d) Review the progress of urban reforms being undertaken by ULBs/Parastatals/implementing agencies.

SLSC shall meet as often as required but shall meet at least thrice in a year without fail and review the progress of ongoing projects and sanction new projects.

Urban Reforms

The main thrust of the revised strategy of urban renewal is to ensure improvement in urban governance so that Urban Local Bodies (ULBs) and parastatal agencies become financially sound with enhanced credit rating and ability to access market capital for undertaking new programmes and expansion of services. In this improved environment, public-private participation models for provisioning of urban amenities would also become feasible. To achieve this objective, state governments, urban local bodies and parastatal agencies will be required to accept implementation of an agenda of reforms. The proposed reforms shall broadly fall into two categories.

(i) Mandatory reforms

(ii) Optional reforms

All the mandatory and optional reforms shall be implemented by the State/ULBs/Parastatals within the scheme period.

Mandatory Reforms

There will be two sets of mandatory reforms. Core reforms at ULB/Parastatal level aiming at process re-engineering through deployment of technology to enable more efficient, reliable, timely services in a transparent manner. The other set of reforms are framework related at state level.

Reforms at Urban Local Body/Parastatal

(i) Adoption of modern, accrual-based double entry system of accounting in urban local bodies/parastatals.

(ii) Introduction of system of e-governance using IT applications like GIS and MIS for various services provided by ULBs/Parastatals.

(iii) Reform of property tax with GIS, so that it becomes major source of revenue for urban local bodies (ULBs) and arrangements for its effective implementation so that collection efficiency reaches at least 85 per cent within next seven years.

(iv) Levy of reasonable user charges by ULBs/Parastatals with the objective that full cost of operation and maintenance, i.e., recurring cost is collected within next seven years. However, cities/towns in North East and other special category states may recover at least 50 per cent of operation and maintenance charges initially. These cities/towns should graduate to full O and M cost recovery in a phased manner.

(v) Internal earmarking within local body, budgets for basic services to the urban poor.

(vi) Provision of basic services to urban poor including security of tenure at affordable prices, improved housing, water supply sanitation and ensuing delivery of other already existing universal services of the government for education, health and social security.

(vii) Assigning or associating elected ULBs with city planning function over a period of seven years, transferring all special agencies that deliver civic services in urban areas to ULBs and creating accountability platforms for all urban civic service providers in transition.

However, in respect of schemes relating to water supply and sanitation, the undermentioned state level mandatory reforms may be taken as optional reforms.

(i) Repeal of Urban Land Ceiling Act.

(ii) Reform of Rent Control Act.

Optional Reforms (State and ULBs/Parastatal Level)

(i) Revision of bye-laws to streamline the approval process for construction of buildings, development of sites, etc.

(ii) Simplification of legal and procedural frameworks for conversion of agricultural land for non-agricultural purposes.

(iii) Introduction of Property Title Certification System in ULBs.

(iv) Earmarking at least 20-25 per cent of developed land in all housing projects (both public and private agencies) for EWS/LIG category with a system of cross subsidisation.

(v) Introduction of computerised process of registration of land and property.

(vi) Revision of bye-laws to make rain water harvesting mandatory in all buildings and adoption of water conservation measures.

(vii) Bye-laws for reuse of recycled water.

(viii) Administrative reforms i.e., reduction in establishment by bringing out voluntary retirement, etc., and achieving specified milestones in this regard.

(ix) Structural reforms.

(x) Encouraging public private partnership.

It is further stipulated that any two optional reforms are to be implemented together by state and ULBs/Parastatals in each year.

Monitoring

(i) Ministry of Urban Development will periodically monitor the scheme through designated officer of this ministry for each state/UT.

(ii) State level nodal agency would send quarterly progress report to the Ministry of Urban Development.

(iii) SLSC would ensure quarterly monitoring of various projects sanctioned under the programme.

(iv) A Monitoring Committee under the chairmanship of Joint Secretary (Urban Development) in the Ministry of

Urban Development would monitor the progress every quarter.

(v) Secretary (UD) would review progress of the programme twice a year.

(vi) TCPO will be responsible for preparing a status report on the scheme in consultation with MOUD every year (by 31st May).

Training and Capacity Building

The central and state governments will make continuous efforts for training and upgradation of the skills of the personnel responsible for the project and the elected representatives. State government may organise suitable training as well as capacity building programmes through reputed institutions in the field. The same will form part of DPR to be submitted by implementing agency.

Memorandum of Agreement (MoA)

Implementation of all mandatory and at least two optional reforms in each year of the scheme by cities/towns will be a condition precedent to access central grant under the scheme. All the reforms (mandatory as well as optional) shall be required to be implemented during the scheme period i.e., seven years. In this regard, the state governments/state level nodal agencies will execute Memorandum of Agreement (MoA) with the Government of India.

(C) Integrated Housing and Slums Development Programme (IHSDP)

IHSDP has been started by merging National Slum Development Programme and Valmiki Ambedkar Housing Plan. The main objective of this programme is to make the cities slums free by providing basic amenities to the slum dwellers. On the basis of 2001 census, this programme will be implemented in cities which have not been covered under JNNURM. Under this programme, the per unit cost of dwelling has been fixed at Rs. 80,000, 80 per cent of which will be the central share and the balance 20 per cent will be contributed by the state government/ local bodies/beneficiaries. Under the scheme, the minimum floor area has been fixed at 25 sq. metres which will include 2 rooms, kitchen and toilet. The beneficiary will have to contribute 12 per cent, but in case of schedule caste/schedule tribes/backward class/other backward castes/handicaped and weaker sections, the contribution may be fixed at 10 per cent. In addition to new construction, there is also a provision of renovations. Preparation of detail project report (DPR) can be outsourced.

Infrastructure Development and Maintenance in the Slums

State governments should ensure a separate provision for upkeep and maintenance of the public assets created under the scheme.

Beneficiary Contribution

Housing should not be provided free to the beneficiaries by the state government. A minimum of 12 per cent beneficiary contribution should be stipulated, which in the case of SC/ST/BC/OBC/PH and other weaker sections shall be 10 per cent.

Admissible Components

(i) Provision of shelter including upgradation and construction of new houses.

(ii) Provision of community toilets.

(iii) Provision of physical amenities like water supply, storm, water drains, community bath, widening and paving of existing lanes, sewers, community latrines, street lights, etc.

(iv) Community infrastructure like provision of community centres to be used for pre-school education, non-formal education, adult education, recreational activities, etc.

(v) Community Primary Health Care Centre Buildings can be provided.

(vi) Social amenities like pre-school education, non-formal education, adult education, maternity, child health and primary health care including immunisation, etc.

(vii) Provision of Model Demonstration Projects.

(viii) Sites and services/houses at affordable costs for EWS and urban poor categories.

(ix) Slum improvement and rehabilitation projects.

(x) Land acquisition cost will not be financed except for acquisition of private land for schemes/projects in the north eastern states and hilly states, viz., Himachal Pradesh, Uttaranchal and Jammu and Kashmir.

DPRs will have to be prepared by the implementing agencies for working under IHSDP including specific project components, viz. health, education and social security. However, the schemes of health, education and social security will be funded through convergence of schemes and detailing of budgetary provisions available under the programmes of the elective sectors (Health, Human Resource Development, Social Justice, Women Empowerment and Labour, etc.), but will also be monitored by the Ministry of Urban Employment and Poverty Alleviation insofar as urban poors are concerned.

The scheme may be converged with other state, sectoral and departmental programmes relating to achieving social sector goals similar to those envisaged in this scheme.

Financing Pattern

The sharing of funds would be in the ratio of 80:20 between central government and state government/ULB/parastatal/states implementing agencies may raise their contribution from their own resources or from beneficiary contribution/financial institutions.

For special category states, the funding pattern between centre and the states will be in the ratio of 90:10.

Funds from MPLAD/MLALD could be canalised towards project cost and to that extent states share could be suitably reduced. However, MPLAD/MLALAD fund would not substitute beneficiary contribution.

The scheme will be implemented through a designated state level nodal agency.

In case Externally Aided Project (EAP) funds are available, these cannot be passed through as ACA (additional centre assistance) to the state government as funds contributed by state/ULBs/Fls.

Release of Central Assistance

Central assistance (grant) released will go directly to the nodal agencies identified by the state government as Additional Central Assistance.

Release of central share to nodal agency will depend on availability of state share and submission of utilisation certificates in accordance with the provisions of General Financial Rules (GFRs).

The criteria for release of funds are as under:

> State share has to be deposited in a separate account to become eligible for the central grant. Fifty per cent of the central grant will be released to the state nodal agency after verification of the state share, and on signing the tripartite Memorandum of Agreement. Second installment will be released based on the progress.

Incentives

After due assessment of status of implementation of activities for which incentives are sought, Central Sanctioning Committee/ State Level Co-ordination Committee may sanction/recommend additional central grant upto a maximum of 10 per cent to incentivise implementing agencies as indicated below:

- For adoption of innovative approaches and adoption of proven and appropriate technologies.
- For information, education and communication (IEC).
- For training and capacity building relating to project/ scheme.
- For preparation of detailed project reports.
- For bringing about efficiencies in the projects.

State Level Nodal Agency

The state government may designate any existing institution as nodal agency for implementation of the scheme.

The nodal agency will be responsible for the following:

- Inviting project proposals from ULBs/implementing agencies.

- Techno-economic appraisal of the projects either through in-house expertise or by outside agencies through outsourcing.
- Management of funds received from central and state governments.
- Disbursement of the funds as per the financing pattern given in the guidelines.
- Furnishing of utilisation certificates, in accordance with the provisions of GFRs and quarterly physical and financial progress reports to the Ministry of Urban Development.
- Maintenance of audited accounts of funds released to ULBs and implementing agencies.

Project Appraisal

Urban Local Bodies and implementing agencies will submit detailed project reports to the designated state level nodal agencies for appraisal.

The state level nodal agency will forward the appraised projects to Ministry of Urban Employment and Poverty Alleviation for consideration of CSC/State Level Co-ordination Committee, as the case may be.

State Level Co-ordination Committee (SLCC)

The composition of the State Level Co-ordination Committee (SLCC) will be decided by the states.

SLCC will ensure the following:

- Examine and approve project reports submitted by the local bodies/implementing agencies taking into account the appraisal reports.
- Periodically monitor the progress of sanctioned projects/ schemes including funds mobilisation from financial institutions.
- Review the implementation of the scheme keeping in view its broad objectives and ensure that the programmes taken up are in accordance with the guidelines laid down.

- Review the progress of urban reforms being undertaken by ULBs/implementing agencies.

Central Sanctioning Committee

The composition of Central Sanctioning Committee (CSC) will be as per the VAMBAY scheme with following composition:

(i) Secretary, UEPA	Chairperson
(ii) Joint Secretary (UEPA)	Member
(iii) JS and FA	Member
(iv) US (UD)	Member
(v) CMD, HUDCO	Member
(vi) Director (UPA)	Member

The CSC will examine and approve the projects relating to housing and integrated projects on housing and infrastructure development, submitted by the state nodal agencies on the recommendations of the state level co-ordination committee.

The state level co-ordination committee will examine and approve the projects relating to providing only basic amenities/ improvements of infrastructure to the slum dwellers.

Agenda of Reforms

The main thrust of the revised strategy of urban renewal including providing basic services to the urban poor (BSUP) is to ensure improvement in urban governance so that urban local bodies (ULBs) and parastatal agencies become financially sound with enhanced credit rating and ability to access market capital for undertaking new programmes and expansion of services. In this improved environment, public-private participation models for provisioning of various services would also become feasible. To achieve this objective, state government, urban local bodies and parastatal agencies will be required to accept implementation of an agenda of reforms. The proposed reforms shall broadly fall into two categories:

(i) Mandatory reforms

(ii) Optional reforms

List of Mandatory and Optional reforms are explained latter.

National Steering Group may add additional reforms to the identified reforms.

The state governments, ULBs and parastatal agencies will be required to execute a Memorandum of Agreement (MoA) with the Government of India committing to implement the reform programme. MoA would also spell out specific milestones to be achieved for each item of reform. Signing of this tripartite MoA will be a necessary condition to access central assistance.

Monitoring

- Ministry of Urban Employment and Poverty Alleviation will periodically monitor the scheme through designated officer of the ministry of each state/UT.
- State level nodal agency would send quarterly progress report to the ministry of MOUEPA.
- SLCC/CSC would ensure quarterly monitoring of various projects recommended/sanctioned under the programme.

Training and Capacity Building

The central and state governments will make continuous efforts for training and upgradation of the skills of the personnel responsible for the project and the elected representatives. State government may organise suitable training as well as capacity building programmes through reputed institutions in the field. The same will form part of DPR to be submitted by implementing agency.

Miscellaneous

It will be the responsibility of urban local bodies/implementing agencies to keep an inventory of assets created and also to maintain and operate the assets and facilities created.

The implementing agencies at the ULB/implementing agency level will be required to open and maintain separate bank account for each project in a commercial bank for receipt and expenditure of all money to be received and spent. ULBs/ implementing agencies should maintain registers for utilisation of funds separately for central and state shares and loan from financial institutions.

The nodal agency will maintain institution-wise and project-wise accounts under the scheme.

Projects taken up under the ongoing schemes under VAMBAY during the last five years beginning from 2001-2002 will continue to be funded as per the existing guidelines of VAMBAY scheme till completion of those projects. Further, till the IHSDP scheme is put in place, even fresh proposals may be taken up under VAMBAY for the year 2005-06.

Ministry of Urban Employment and Poverty Alleviation, in consultation with Ministry of Finance, may effect changes in the scheme guidelines, other than those affecting the financing pattern as the scheme proceeds, if such changes are considered necessary.

Urban Reforms

Urban reforms may include:

Mandatory Reforms

Urban Local Body Reforms (at ULBs' Level)

(i) Adoption of modern accrual-based double entry system of accounting in urban local bodies.

(ii) Introduction of system of e-governance using IT applications like GIS and MIS for various services provided by ULBs.

(iii) Reform of property tax with GIS, so that it becomes major source of revenue for urban local bodies (ULBs) and arrangements for its effective implementation so that collection efficiency reaches at least 85 per cent within next five years.

(iv) Levy of reasonable user charges by ULBs/Parastatals with the objective that full cost of operation and maintenance is collected within next five years. However, cities/towns in North-East and other special category states may recover at least 50 per cent of operation and maintenance charges in city. These cities/towns should graduate to full O and M cost recovery in a phased manner.

(v) Internal earmarking within local body budgets for basic services to the urban poor.

(vi) Provision of basic services to urban poor including security of tenure at affordable prices, improved housing, water supply, sanitation and ensuring delivery of other already existing universal services of the government, e.g., free education, healthy and social security.

State Level Reforms

(i) Implementation of decentralisation measures as envisaged in Seventy-fourth Constitution Amendment. States should ensure meaningful association/engagement of ULBs in planning function of parastatals as well as delivery of services for the citizens.

(ii) Rationalisation of stamp duty to bring it down to not more than 5 per cent within next five years.

(iii) Enactment of community participation law to institutionalise citizen participation and introducing the concept of the Area Sabha in urban areas.

(iv) Assigning or associating elected ULBs into "city planning function" over a period of five years; transferring all special agencies that deliver civic services in urban areas and creating accountability platforms for all urban civic service providers in transition.

Optional Reforms

(i) Repeal of Urban Land Ceiling and Regulation Act.

(ii) Amendment of Rent Control laws balancing the interest of landlords and tenants.

(iii) Enactment of Public Disclosure Law to ensure preparation of medium term fiscal plan of ULBs and release of quarterly performance information to all stakeholders.

(iv) Revision of bye-laws to streamline the approval process for construction of buildings, development of sites, etc.

(v) Simplification of legal and procedural frameworks for conversion of agricultural land for non-agricultural purposes.

(vi) Introduction of Property Title Certification System in ULBs.

(vii) Earmarking at least 20-25 per cent of developed land in all housing projects (both public and private agencies) for EWS/LIG category with a system of cross subsidisation.

(viii) Introduction of computerised process of registration of land and property.

(ix) Revision of bye-laws to make rain water harvesting mandatory in all buildings to come up in future and for adoption of water conservation measures.

(x) Bye-laws on reuse of recycled water.

(xi) Administrative reforms, i.e., reduction in establishment by bringing out voluntary retirement schemes, non-filling up of posts falling vacant due to retirement, etc. and achieving specified milestones in this regard.

(xii) Structural reforms.

(xiii) Encouraging public-private partnership.

State/ULBs are further required to implement the mandatory reforms and optional reforms within the Mission period. The states/ULBs need to choose at least two optional reforms each year for implementation. The details of reforms which have already been implemented and/or proposed to be taken up should be included in the detailed project reports.

Summary and Recommendations

6

Privatisation drive started after the adoption of New Economic Policy in 1991, has slowly and steadily percolated upto the level of local self-government in general and the urban local bodies (ULBs) in particular. In this context, many urban local bodies are reported to have privatised the collection of certain sources of revenue and expenditure items. A particular mention here may be made of the collection of octroi, the provision of streetlighting, collection of garbage, etc. It was reported that the collection of revenue from octroi had substantially increased after privatisation. But at the same time, certain loopholes and malpractices had come to the light. Similar results could be expected if the collection of other municipal taxes like house tax is also privatised. Therefore, the major objective of the study was to examine the actual or potential increase in revenue from different sources particularly after privatisation.

A similar impact can also be expected if the provision of different municipal services like streetlighting, sanitation, water supply, sewerage, etc. are also privatised. To what extent, the privatisation of services would improve their quality and coverage was another objective of the study. The study is all the more important in view of the fact that the proportion of urban population in the country has been increasing and in the wake of 74th Constitutional Amendment already 18 functions, stand to be transferred to ULBs.

The specific objectives of the study were:

1. To examine the change in revenue from different sources after privatisation in the ULBs in the selected states.

2. To examine the efficiency of different municipal services after privatisation in the selected states.
3. To examine the implications, including the reduction of staff requirements, after the provision of privatising certain services in ULBs.
4. In the light of above objectives the study was to identify the activities or part of activities that may be taken up for privatisation by ULBs.

The study is based mostly on the secondary data collected from some selected municipalities/corporations. Field surveys were also conducted in some of the states notably, Punjab, Haryana, Uttarakhand, Andhra Pradesh, Himachal Pradesh, etc.

Some of the important findings of the study are summarised as below:

> Many ULBs have tried successfully to privatise their revenue sources, notably octroi collections. Even the collection of property tax has been seen to have improved by involving the stakeholders (property owners) in self-assessment of property tax, thereby making the municipal officials responsible for levying the property tax redundant. However, it must be mentioned that although privatisation of octroi collection has many advantages yet it has to be handled cautiously. After privatisation of octroi some complaints of harassment by contractors are also received. Thus, strict vigil and monitoring is needed in this arrangement by the concerned official agencies in order to avoid the above situation. Revenue from octroi increased in almost all the municipalities after the contract system and on the other hand expenditure on octroi staff and patrolling was substantially reduced.

Similarly, the experience of Bengaluru Municipal Corporation shows that reposing faith in property owners i.e., self-assessment of property tax can greatly improve its collections. Property tax collections nearly increased three times between 1999-2000 and 2006-07, i.e., after the self-assessment of property tax was made mandatory and some rebate was given to those who paid the tax in advance. It may be interesting to observe that since the value of property determines one's ability to pay tax, therefore, it may be significant to examine the relationship between value of property and property tax; and between urban development and value of property.

It has been found that value of property and property tax are inversely related, i.e., as property tax increases, value of property decreases and *vice versa*. Therefore, whenever the value of property is enhanced by spending more and more on urban infrastructure or by providing other urban amenities as is the case with Jawaharlal Nehru National Urban Renewable Mission (JNNURM), then the prospects of raising more resources through property tax are also enhanced. It should be remembered that enhanced value of property is unearned income/wealth, therefore, on equity ground also property tax should be made more progressive.

On the other hand, as higher property tax rates lower the value of property, therefore, the tax proceeds should be used to enhance the municipal infrastructure, thereby increasing the value of property to neutralise this adverse effect.

The foremost problem in ULBs is the littering away and dumping of all types of waste on the roads, streets, drains and other public places. The management of solid wastes is one of the essential services and it is obligatory duty of urban local bodies to arrange for daily cleaning, collection, transportation, processing and disposal of wastes. Proper discharge of this service is essential to public health, a clean environment and good healthy living. Due to lack of appropriate efforts by local authorities and apathy on the part of citizens, solid waste management has become a tenacious problem and this has happened, not withstanding the fact that the largest part of municipal expenditure is allocated to it. Even the Twelfth Finance Commission has asked the municipal bodies to spend at least 50 per cent of the enhanced grants (Rs. 5,000 crores) on solid waste management.

In this contest one can learn a lot from the southern states which have applied the various strategies to convert 'trash to cash' and 'waste to wealth'. The 'people participatory approach' of Suryapet (A.P.) and 'public-private partnership' of Namakkal (T.N.) are worth emulating. While the former implies the change of mindset of all the stakeholders (NGOs, people and the municipal staff including municipal councillors), the latter approach lays stress on privatisation right at the door to door collection with segregation at source into organic and inorganic wastes. Then, on BOT principle the former (organic) waste is converted into vermi compost and the latter into recyclable waste and inorganic waste.

The most striking success has been achieved in Greater Visakhapatnam Corporation (A.P.) which, with 15 lakh population, daily generates 750 metric tonnes of solid waste. But with privatisation drive, it has ensured 24 hours cleanliness in the city. The most hazardous bio-medical waste is disposed of through scientific methods with no adverse effect on environment.

However, it must be stated that the municipal councillors in the above mentioned towns in southern states have played a commendable role. By adopting a scheme of 'recognition and awards' for the achievers and 'fines and penalties' for the defaulters, these municipal bodies have achieved the status of 'dustbin free' and 'zero garbage' towns.

In respect of streetlighting, it was found that prior to privatisation, Municipal Corporation of Patiala (Punjab) had to incur Rs. 13 per point on maintenance cost, but after the privatisation maintenance cost was reduced to Rs. 6.50 per point. Whereas prior to privatisation, 60-70 per cent of the streetlight points were functional, but after the privatisation 90-95 per cent of the points became functional as the contractor could be held responsible for the non-functioning of the streetlight points. As per the agreement clause, the contractor would ensure that no streetlight point remained out of order for more than 24 hours from the receipts/registration of complaint in the corporation/contractor's office. If the contractor defaults to maintain the streetlight properly or is unable to replace the defective points within 24 hours, he can be penalised as per agreed clause. But prior to privatisation, no one could be held responsible for the non-functioning of the streetlight points and on the other hand there was no proper patrolling for monitoring the working of the streetlights. However, some people complained that there was not much improvement in the functioning of streetlight in their areas even after privatisation, because the contractor tended to concentrate mostly in VIP areas. Generally, people are of the view that privatisation is better if proper checking and monitoring of the work done by the contractor is held regularly.

Similarly, the operation of other services can also improve through privatisation provided there is proper monitoring by the citizens and appropriate clause of fine for the defaulter is incorporated in MoU. However, in case of better performance the efforts of the service providers should be suitably acknowledged/awarded.

Recently, the Union Government has introduced many schemes such as Jawaharlal Nehru National Urban Renewable Mission (JNNURM), Urban Infrastructure Development Schemes for Small and Medium Towns (UIDSSMT), Integrated Housing and Slums Development Programme (IHSDP), etc. to persuade the states and ULBs to adopt a rights-based approach for affordable housing, sanitation, water supply, sewerage, etc. and for providing a clean environment to all urban dwellers. Further to make the schemes sustainable, it is a happy augury that the central schemes like JNNURM has made it mandatory to impose property tax. Many states like Punjab, which had exempted all the residential properties (irrespective of the size) from paying the property tax have already decided to impose it. In the long run, it is only the property tax and levying user's charges on urban amenities that can sustain the fiscal health of ULBs. Indirect taxes, like octroi and entry tax apart from being regressive, are inconsistent in a Value Added Tax system.

In the course of study it was found that some states like Uttarakhand have yet to take some concrete steps to transfer the routine services like streetlighting, drinking water, sewerage, etc. to ULBs. These services are still being continued to be operated by the parent departments of the state government, which has belittled the importance of municipal bodies. Therefore, the 13th Finance Commission must see to it that mere enactment of 73rd and 74th Constitutional Amendments is not a sufficient indicator to ensure the functional and financial autonomy for the institutions of Local Self-Government.

Further in order to encourage municipalities to build infrastructure, some in-built mechanism to ensure regular and ever increasing transfer of resources to municipalities must be there. Ad hoc grants, even if substantial are not conducive to the growth of urban infrastructure.

Appendix

Rural-Urban Distribution of Population in Indian States/ Union Territories, 2001

Territory	T/R/U	Persons	Males	Females	Percentage of Urban population
India	T	1,027,015,247	531,277,078	495,738,169	27.8
	R	741,660,293	381,141,184	360,519,109	
	U	285,354,954	150,135,894	135,219,060	
State/Union Territory					
Jammu and Kashmir	T	10,069,917	5,300,574	4,796,343	24.9
	R	7,564,608	3,925,846	3,638,762	
	U	2,505,309	1,374,728	1,130,581	
Himachal Pradesh	T	6,077,248	3,085,256	1,130,581	9.8
	R	5,482,367	2,754,251	2,728,116	
	U	594,881	331,005	263,876	
Punjab	T	24,289,296	12,963,362	11,325,934	34.0
	R	16,043,730	8,500,647	7,543,083	
	U	8,245,566	4,462,715	3,782,851	
Chandigarh*	T	900,914	508,224	392,690	89.8
	R	92,118	56,837	35,281	
	U	808,796	451,387	357,409	
Uttarakhand	T	8,479,562	4,316,401	4,163,161	25.6
	R	6,309,317	3,143,380	3,165,937	
	U	2,170,245	1,173,021	997,224	
Haryana	T	21,082,989	11,327,658	9,755,531	29.0
	R	14,968,850	8,017,622	6,951,228	
	U	6,114,139	3,310,036	2,804,103	

(Contd.)

Territory	T/R/U	Persons	Males	Females	Percentage of Urban population
Delhi*	T	13,782,976	7,570,890	6,212,086	93.0
	R	963,215	533,219	429,996	
	U	12,819,761	7,037,671	5,782,090	
Rajasthan	T	56,473,122	29,381,657	27,091,465	23.4
	R	43,267,678	22,394,479	20,873,199	
	U	13,205,444	6,987,178	6,218,266	
Uttar Pradesh	T	166,052,859	87,466,301	78,586,558	20.8
	R	131,540,230	69,096,765	62,443,465	
	U	34,512,629	18,369,536	16,143,093	
Bihar	T	82,878,796	43,153,964	39,724,832	10.5
	R	74,199,596	38,510,686	35,688,910	
	U	8,679,200	4,643,278	4,035,922	
Sikkim	T	540,493	228,217	252,276	11.1
	R	480,488	225,386	225,102	
	U	60,005	32,831	27,174	
Arunachal Pradesh	T	1,091,117	573,951	517,166	20.4
	R	868,429	453,560	414,869	
	U	222,688	120,391	102,297	
Nagaland	T	1,988,636	1,041,686	946,950	17.7
	R	1,635,815	846,651	789,164	
	U	352,821	195,035	157,786	
Manipur	T	2,388,634	1,207,338	1,181,296	23.9
	R	1,818,224	923,428	894,796	
	U	570,410	283,910	286,500	
Mizoram	T	891,058	459,783	431,275	49.5
	R	450,018	233.718	216.300	
	U	441,040	226,065	214,975	
Tripura	T	3,191,168	1,636,138	155,030	17.0
	R	2,648,074	1,359,288	1,288,786	
	U	543,094	276,850	266,244	
Meghalaya	T	2,306,069	1,167,840	1,138,229	19.6
	R	1,853,457	939,803	913,654	
	U	452,612	228,037	224,575	
Assam	T	26,638,407	13,787,799	12,850,608	12.7
	R	23,248,994	11,983,157	11,265,837	
	U	3,389,413	1,804,672	1,584,771	

(Contd.)

Territory	T/R/U	Persons	Males	Females	Percentage of Urban population
West Bengal	T	80,221,171	41,487,694	38,733,477	28.0
	R	57,734,690	29,606,028	2,812,662	
	U	22,486,481	11,881,666	10,604,815	
Jharkhand	T	26,909,428	13,861,277	13,048,151	22.3
	R	20,922,731	10,660,430	10,262,301	
	U	5,986,697	3,200,847	2,785,850	
Orissa	T	36,706,920	18,612,340	18,094,580	15.0
	R	31,210,602	15,711,853	15,498,749	
	U	5,496,318	2,900,487	2,595,831	
Chhattisgarh	T	20,795,956	10,452,426	10,343,530	20.1
	R	16,620,627	8,290,983	8,329,644	
	U	4,175,329	2,161,443	2,013,886	
Madhya Pradesh	T	60,385,118	31,456,873	28,928,245	26.7
	R	44,282,528	22,975,256	21,307,272	
	U	16,102,590	8,481,617	7,620,973	
Gujarat	T	50,596,992	26,344,053	24,252,239	37.4
	R	31,697,615	16,289,423	15,408,192	
	U	18,899,377	10,054,630	8,844,747	
Daman and Diu*	T	1,580,559	92,478	65,581	36.3
	R	100,740	63,576	37,164	
	U	57,319	28,902	28,417	
Dadra and Nagar Haveli*	T	220,451	121,731	98,720	22.9
	R	169,995	91,887	78,108	
	U	50,456	29,844	20,612	
Maharashtra	T	96,752,247	50,334,270	46,417,977	42.4
	R	55,732,513	28,443,238	27,289,275	
	U	41,019,734	21,891,032	19,128,702	
Andhra Pradesh	T	75,727,541	38,286,811	37,440,730	27.1
	R	55,223,944	27,852,179	27,371,765	
	U	20,503,597	10,434,632	10,068,965	
Karnataka	T	52,733,958	26,856,343	25,877,615	34.0
	R	34,814,100	17,618,593	17,195,507	
	U	17,919,858	9,237,750	8,682,108	

(Contd.)

Territory	T/R/U	Persons	Males	Females	Percentage of Urban population
Goa	T	1,343,998	685,617	658,381	49.8
	R	675,129	339,626	335,503	
	U	668,869	345,991	322,878	
Lakshadweep*	T	60,595	31,118	29,477	44.5
	R	33,647	17,196	16,451	
	U	26,948	13,922	13,026	
Kerala	T	31,838,619	15,468,646	16,369,955	26.0
	R	23,571,484	11,450,785	12,120,699	
	U	8,267,135	4,017,879	4,249,256	
Tamil Nadu	T	62,110,839	31,268,654	30,842,185	43.9
	R	34.879,286	17,508,985	17,360,301	
	U	27,241,553	13,759,669	13,481,884	
Pondicherry*	T	973,829	486,705	487,124	66.6
	R	325,596	163,586	162,010	
	U	648,233	323,119	325,114	
Andaman and Nicobar Islands*	T	356,265	192,985	163,280	32.7
	R	239,858	128,837	111,021	
	U	116,407	64,148	52,259	

Source: Registrar General Census (2001).

T = Total, R = Rural and U = Urban

*Union Territory

References

Adhia, Hasmukh: One-Day Governance: The Gujarat Experience, in *Learn From Them: A Compilation of Best Practices,* Penguin Books India, New Delhi, 2007.

Chauhan, Uttara and Niraj Lal: "Public-Private Partnerships for Urban Poor in Ahmedabad: A Slum Project", *Economic and Political Weekly,* March 6-13, 1999.

Dutta, Shyam, S.: "Partnerships in Urban Development: A Review of Ahmedabad's Experience", *Environment and Urbanization,* Vol. 12 (1), 2000.

Dhanija, Urvashi: *Sustainable Solid Waste Management: Issues Policies and Structure,* Academic Foundation, New Delhi, 2006.

Gaikwad, Ratnakar: 'City Wide Sanitation, Pune Experience', in *Learn From Them: A Compilation Best Practices,* Penguin Books India, New Delhi, 2007.

Government of India: Report of the Eleventh Finance Commission, New Delhi, 2000.

Government of India: Report of the Twelfth Finance Commission, New Delhi, 2004.

Government of Punjab: Various Issues of Statistical Abstract of Punjab.

Government of Punjab: *Report of the First Finance Commission*, Chandigarh, December, 1995.

Government of Punjab: *Report of the Second Finance Commission,* Chandigarh, February, 2002.

Government of Punjab: *Report of the Third Finance Commission (Interim Report,* Chandigarh, January, 2006.

Gupta, K.R. (Ed.): *Urban Development Debates, Volume 1-4,* Atlantic Publishers, 2005.

Kundu, A., Bagchi, S. and Kundu, D.: "Regional Distribution of Infrastructure and Basic Amenities in Urban India: Issues Concerning Empowerment of Local Bodies", *Economic and Political Weekly,* 34 (28), 1999.

National Council of Applied Economic Research: "A Study of the Resources of Municipal Bodies", New Delhi, April, 1960.

National Institute of Urban Affairs: *The Nature and Dimensions of Urban Fiscal Crisis*, Research study series No. 18, New Delhi, February, 1987.

National Institute of Urban Affairs: *Upgrading Municipal Services Norm and Financial Implication*, Vol. I, Research study series No. 38, New Delhi, 1989.

National Institute of Urban Affairs: *Public-Private Provision of Urban Service*, Research study series No. 50, New Delhi, December, 1992.

National Institute of Urban Affairs: *Scope and Practice of Privatisation of Urban Services in India*, Research study series No. 60, New Delhi, December, 1997.

National Institute of Urban Affairs: *Abolition of Octroi—A Study of its Impact on Municipal Finance and Transport Efficiency*, Research study serial No. 68 New Delhi, January, 1998.

Patel, Sujata and Saskia Sassen: "Cities Today: A New Frontier", *The Urban Age*, Vol. 4, No. 1, May, 1996.

Peterson, George, E. and Patricia Clarke Annez: *Financing Cities*, Sage Publications, New Delhi, 2007.

Rao, S. Bhoopathi and Abdul Sameen Ansari: *Solid Waste Management in Urban Local Bodies: The Indian Experience*, Osmania University, Hyderabad, 2005.

Sarin, Rahul: "Introduction: Learning From Best Practices" in *Learn From Them: A Compilation Best Practices*, Penguin Books India, New Delhi, 2007.

Sharma, Veena: "Sources of Municipal Revenue With Special Reference to Property Tax—A Case Study of Punjab", Unpublished Ph.D. thesis, Punjabi University, Patiala, 1999.

Singh, U.B.: *Urban Administration in India (Experience of Fifty Years)*, Serials Publications, New Delhi, 2004.

